OUR BIG FAT CAMPERVAN ROAD TRIP

Part One: To The Arctic Circle and Back

Chris Wise

Mandrill Media

Copyright © 2004 Chris Wise

Our Big Fat Campervan Road Trip
Part One: To The Arctic Circle and Back

ISBN: 9781998998517

Published by Mandrill Media. 128 The Mount, York, YO24 1AS.
Contact: chris.wise@mandrillmedia.tv

All rights reserved. No part of this book may be reproduced in any form by electronic or mechanical means, including information storage and retrieval systems, without permission in writing from the publisher, except by a reviewer who may quote brief passages for the purposes of a review in accordance with accepted fair dealing principles provided always that the author and publisher are credited. The moral rights of the author have been asserted.

All trademarks appearing in this book are the property of their respective owners. They are included for the convenience of readers and to make the book more complete. They should not be construed as endorsements from, or of any of these third parties or their products or services.

All photographs remain the copyright of the author.

Cover Illustration by Ellie Lewis

DISCLAIMER

This book is a general guide to taking a campervan or motorhome road trip in Europe. It's the author's personal experiences and opinions from his own campervan adventure. The content provided is for information and entertainment only.

While every effort has been made to include accurate and up-to-date information, the publisher and the author assume no responsibility for any inaccuracies, errors, omissions, or inconsistencies in the content of this book, and hereby disclaim any liability to any party for any loss, damage, or disruption caused by errors or omissions, whether such errors or omissions result from negligence, accident, or any other cause.

This book includes location details for parking and overnight stopovers. While the author has taken great care to observe the laws in all the countries he visited, he is not a lawyer. The laws, rules, permissions and charges for parking in specific locations can change. The publisher and author make no warranty that parking or overnight camping at locations referred to in this book is legal. It is the reader's responsibility to check a country's laws, and local rules and regulations at the time they travel.

This publication is meant as a source of valuable information for the reader, however it is not meant as a substitute for direct expert assistance. If such level of assistance is required, the services of a competent professional should be sought.

This book contains links and references to websites and organisations which are owned and operated by third parties. These are included for information and convenience only. The publisher and author have no control over the operation and content of these websites and organisations and make no warranties about the information contained in them. If you access any third-party websites, you do so entirely at your own risk.

The publisher and author are providing this book and its content on an "as is" basis. Your use of the information in this book is at your own risk, and your use of this book implies your acceptance of this disclaimer.

CONTENTS

Title Page
Copyright
1. Leaving It All Behind — 1
2. Going Dutch — 6
3. Hamelin and Hamburg — 11
4. How Swedish are We! — 19
5. Island Hopping and Discovering Stockholm — 25
6. Wilderness Camping and a Plague of Frogs — 31
7. The Swedish High Coast — 36
8. Spectacular Norway and The Midnight Sun — 42
9. Tromsø – Gateway to the Arctic — 46
10. The Lofoten Islands — 51
11. Vikings, Gales, and a Roadside Rescue — 56
12. The Arctic Circle Centre & Trondheim treats — 62
13. Drives of our Lives — 68
14. Mountain Climbing in a Campervan — 74
15. The Mega-tunnel and The Snow Road — 79
16. Dinosaurs and Deep-Sea Disasters — 85
17. Floating Saunas and £12 pints — 90
18. The Road to Gothenburg — 96
19. Wonderful Copenhagen — 103
20. Hamlet's Castle and Cold War Chills — 109
21. Onwards to Odense — 115
22. LEGO®Town Joys and a Taste of The Sahara — 120

23. Old Town Ribe and a Brand-New Beach	127
24. Rotterdam Revelations	131
Appendix 1	139
With Thanks...	141
About The Author	143
Books By This Author	145

1. LEAVING IT ALL BEHIND

We weren't total vanlife virgins when we rolled up at the ferry terminal in Harwich to embark on our big fat campervan adventure. But our most ambitious expedition before then had been spending Christmas at a very moist campsite in Weston Super Mare. Hardly preparation for the year-long tour of Europe that was about to begin.

As we joined a queue of campervans and motorhomes inching towards passport control, it felt unreal. Covid had delayed our once-in-a-lifetime road trip for over two years. We'd re-scheduled so many times it was hard to believe our adventure was finally happening. And even though we'd lived with the idea of our expedition for ages, it was still a huge deal for folks like us.

Gap years hadn't been invented when we left school. Steve and I had both gone straight into jobs. Sure, we'd enjoyed family holidays, but nothing on the scale of the trip that, in our minds, would start the second we cleared border control.

We pulled up to the barrier and presented our passports for inspection. Why did I feel so guilty? Logically, I knew a forensic search of our camper would reveal no trace of weapons, drugs, booze, or stowaways. Fingers crossed, our giant bag of over one thousand

1

Yorkshire Tea bags wouldn't raise too many suspicions either. But I still had a knot in my stomach when the border official asked the purpose of our trip.

"Well officer, we have just walked out on our everyday lives. We've abandoned our loved ones to fend for themselves. We have no detailed plan of where we're going and have made a pact not to give a fig about anything or anyone for at least twelve months."

That may not be exactly how we phrased it, but it's how it felt. The explanation must have met official approval because the border guard stamped our passports and waived us through the barrier towards the ferry.

Maybe I was apprehensive because our impending adventure was risky. We'd both walked away from our jobs with the NHS. We'd packed up our home and put all our worldly goods in storage – apart from the essentials we'd crammed into our van. (Far more pants, T-shirts, and towels than humans need to function - as it turned out.)

I can't deny that excitement kicked in as we drove up the giant ramp and into the cavernous belly of the good ship Stena Hollandica. But our joy at finally being underway was tinged with worries about money.

Money Matters

After buying and equipping our campervan, we had no savings; apart from a few hundred pounds generously gifted by guests at our wedding only a month earlier. This was going to be the mother of all honeymoons too.

Our grand plan had always been to fund our trip by renting out our flat for a year. The rental income had to cover everything: food and drink; fuel and LPG gas; road and bridge tolls; ferry crossings; emergency van repairs and admissions to attractions.

Preparations had been stacking up nicely until a week before our departure. Our estate agent had found a faith healer who wanted to be our tenant. Let's just say, the deal fell through at the eleventh hour.

As we stood at the blunt end of the ferry, watching the delights of Harwich disappear in our wake, we had enough money to travel for about a month. After the faith healer disaster, I'd managed to generate some cash by all but giving my old Mini away to an online car dealer.

After checking in to our cabin, we treated ourselves to breakfast in the on-board restaurant. Top Tip: ferry breakfasts are moderately less extortionate if you book them in advance.

The previous months had been chaos. Despite weeks of preparation, we ended up packing right up to the wire. Now, with a seven-hour crossing to The Hook of Holland stretching out in front of us, we could finally absorb the enormity of what we'd done.

Going With The Flow

We'd booked a campsite near the Hook for our first two nights abroad. A chance to acclimatise, recover, re-group, and practise driving on the wrong side of the road. But apart from the campsite reservation and our return ferry three months down the line, our diaries were empty.

For the first time ever, my trusty, obstinately non-digital, A4, week-to-view, paper diary had page after page of absolutely zilch. Some might find that liberating. As a self-confessed control freak, it left me feeling ever so slightly sick.

But we had a sworn agreement. This trip was about making it up as we went along. I'd committed to not planning in detail and was under oath to go with the flow. (If you think you just heard a faint scream, it came from somewhere deep inside me as I typed that last sentence.)

When our ferry docked at The Hook of Holland, the route of our up-coming road trip existed in the vaguest, viewed-from-space level of detail.

Our idea was to scoot quickly east across Holland and Germany and take another ferry over the Baltic Sea to Trelleborg on the southern tip of Sweden. Then, we'd drive north up the eastern coast of ABBAland, sneak into Finland and head west into Norway. Exploring Norway's Lofoten islands was a must because we'd seen how amazing they looked on YouTube.

Next, we'd head south through Norway and pop briefly into western Sweden before taking that enormous bridge (star of that great Scandi police series) across to Denmark. After exploring Daneland, we'd hurry back through Germany and Holland to catch our ferry back to the UK.

As for the day-to-day details – they'd depend entirely on where 'Cliff', our trusty campervan, would take us.

Big Trip Inspiration

This book follows our adventures on that first leg of our grand tour – a three-month, seven-thousand-mile (11,000 km) round trip from the UK, well into the Artic Circle and back.

It's an honest, purely personal account of the places we discovered. A friendly travelogue that could inspire you to follow in our tyre tracks – even for just part of our route.

I've included pin-point accurate 'what3words' location details for over 150 places we parked our camper. These include useful parking places for visiting towns, cities, and attractions, the official campsites we used, and the most idyllic wilderness locations where we spent the night. The references look like this; (///three.words.here). What3words is simple to use, integrates with Google Maps and is accurate to within three square metres. You'll find a simple guide to using it in Appendix 1.

If you've never considered travelling in a campervan or motorhome, prepare to be converted. If you already own a mobile home, you'll discover some amazing places to take it.

Eventually, we *did* spend a life-changing twelve months exploring

Europe in our van. Taking our accommodation with us allowed us to tick off countless destinations and attractions that had been on our bucket lists for years.

But more importantly, it gave us the privilege of experiencing some of Europe's truly spectacular locations that are not, and never will be on, the usual tourist trail.

2. GOING DUTCH

I've mentioned that we christened our campervan 'Cliff'. I don't understand why this made our friends snigger. It had nothing to do with the film where Cliff Richard drives around Europe in a London Transport double-decker bus. No, our Cliff is *a* CLIFF – a six-metre, Sunlight Cliff 600 Adventure to be precise. "CLIFF" was emblazoned in big red letters on his flanks when we bought him. So what else were we going to call him! Am I sounding a touch defensive?

As we drove Cliff off the ferry at the Hook of Holland, we found ourselves in our second passport queue of the day. We were about to enter the European Union for the first time since our nation voted to have nothing more to do with it.

Thankfully, the Dutch border guard didn't take it personally and stamped our passports, marking our official entry into the so-called 'Schengen Zone'. The implications of this would become all too clear and rather serious later in our trip.

Steve, my recently acquired Hubster, took the first turn at driving on the right. But he only had to concentrate on avoiding swarms of cyclists and veering over the edge of dykes for fifteen minutes before we arrived at our campsite.

The Strandpark Vlugtenburg (What3words reference - /// photo.cased.provide) is more family holiday park than campsite. It's well equipped and separated from the nearby beach by sand dunes. We found our pitch, enjoyed a celebratory pint at the site's beach bar and took a stroll on the very windy sands, buzzed by kitesurfers.

Bank Card Bother

Next morning, we needed supplies. A thirty-minute walk to the nearest Hoogvliet supermarket confirmed the cliché that everyone in The Netherlands travels by bicycle. We narrowly escaped being mowed down several times because we couldn't distinguish bike lanes from footpaths. It didn't help that most cycling Netherlanders seemed to travel in packs, deep in conversation as they pedalled.

Having reached the safety of the supermarket, we did that very Brits abroad thing. We mooched along the aisles, smiling smugly at brands we recognised - sniggering to hide our ignorance when we came across products from other planets.

Techmeister Steve saved the day with the Google Lens app on his phone. He selected 'translate' and pointed his camera at the packaging. Magically, the app superimposed English words over the Dutch gobbledygook on his screen. Trust me, it's the easiest way to distinguish your stroopwafels from your speculaas.

However, hi-tech translation didn't prepare us for what happened at the checkout. This Dutch supermarket chain didn't accept Visa or Mastercard (though I believe the policy may have changed since our visit). Even our new joint Starling bank account, set up specially to avoid overseas transaction and currency conversion charges, was rejected. The store manager explained they only accepted Maestro cards which, if I'm not mistaken, disappeared from Britain in Victorian times.

A friendly checkout operator allowed us to stash our shopping behind the till until we returned with some euros that we managed to wrestle from cash point down the street.

It wasn't a great start to day one. However, I should mention that our bank card didn't let us down in the other nineteen countries we'd eventually visit on our travels – and we did use it in some very unusual places. Top Tip: always carry a little local currency in case of card emergencies.

Delightful Delft

Day two dawned bright and sunny so I persuaded Steve that we should go to Delft. I'd visited the city decades earlier to interview Doctor Death. He was well-respected hospital doctor and a strong advocate of voluntary euthanasia. He'd helped many of his terminally ill patients to die – only those who wanted to, and all within Dutch law, I hasten to add. But that was in my distant days as a current affairs reporter. I was determined my return visit to Delft would have a lighter feel.

First, we faced what would become a familiar challenge when visiting cities – finding somewhere to park. There's only one way to put this. Many towns and cities don't like campervans and motorhomes. Historic, tourist hotspots tend to be the most hostile.

It can be stressful driving a large vehicle through narrow streets you don't know. Height barriers and tight spaces can turn parking into a nightmare. That's if you can find a car park that allows campers in the first place. We adopted an approach to take the hassle out of visiting built-up areas; find free parking on the outskirts and take public transport or walk to the centre.

An internet search for "free camper parking in Delft" conjured up a spot just twenty minutes' walk out of the city, beside one of its main canals (///bench.chef.rehearsal). As we locked the van, I noticed we'd stopped right beside a sign that declared "No Parking". However, the notice board faced across the water, so we chose to believe it was targeted at boats and barges. We left Cliff where he was and sauntered off towards the city centre.

Delft proved to be a delight. There's far more to it than souvenir shops crammed with that blue and white porcelain beloved by everyone's granny. Streets around the main square had the coolest of Art Deco interior design shops, an entire store dedicated to the cartoon character Tintin and a truly magnificent cheese emporium.

But what really made our visit special was unexpectedly hitting on the Knapsack Festival. Musicians from rock bands to opera singers floated along the canals on barges, pausing to entertain crowds gathered on the banks and bridges. Some bands entertained in the squares and narrow streets. Something in the air seemed to encourage a great deal of dancing. I thought I could smell it.

I've since discovered the festival was quietly euthanised after our visit because it ran out of money. I hope it's resurrected because it made Delft feel young, vibrant, and ever so slightly bonkers.

We wrapped up our visit with a short walk to Delft's Botanical Gardens (///welfare.laptop.contain). They're more research centre than tourist attraction, with a collection of rare trees, plants, and shrubs on a two-acre site at Delft University. The hot house alone was worth the €6 entrance fee.

Ice Cream, Fire And Tornados

We'd never intended to explore much of Holland. As it's one of the closest countries to home, we reckoned it would be easy to return to in the future. So, the next day, we cracked on, heading east towards Germany.

Steve had booked our next overnight near the village-sized city of Borculo, close to the German border. Any self-respecting campervanner would have picked the Camperpark 't Dommerhalt because of its sustainability credentials (///rheumatoid.riot.doses).

Its ten campervan pitches supply electricity from solar panels. It also claims the Netherland's first charging point for electric campervans.

However, the site's planet-saving credentials played no part in Steve's choice. It was entirely to down to it being attached to a farm with an ice cream parlour offering two hundred flavours of ice-cream.

Although we'd never heard of Borculo, it turned out to be a fascinating place to visit. Fascinating, that is, if you get the least bit excited by fire engines.

Borculo has turned its old school into an International Fire Brigade Museum - no less (///entertainer.prescribed.cafe). The "Brandweermuseum" is much more interesting than it sounds. Seriously. We spent a slightly nerdy couple of hours filling our fireman's boots with everything from replicas of seventeenth century fire appliances, hundreds of helmets, hand pumps, horse-drawn pumps and – wait for it - an entire room filled with antique fire extinguishers, many of which were surprisingly attractive. What *am* I saying!

The undoubted stars of the show were more than twenty, beautifully preserved twentieth century fire engines. It's not the dusty, dead museum you might expect. It illustrates the complete history of firefighting and will appeal to anyone who's the least bit interested in vehicles or technology. The displays also include hundreds of diecast model fire trucks and every LEGO® fire engine produced since the fifties. So, kids will get fired up about it too.

One room in the museum is dedicated to what Borculo is most famous for – being all but flattened by a freak tornado on August 10th, 1925. The twister wreaked havoc, killing four people, destroying buildings and tipping over trains. The museum has many photos of the devastation left by what is an incredibly rare weather event in this part of Europe.

3. HAMELIN AND HAMBURG

A short distance out of Borculo we crossed the border into Germany. No passport checks. No barriers. No awkward questions about smuggling teabags. In truth, the border was so low-key we almost missed it.

A couple of stretches of German autobahn sped us on our way to our next campsite – Campingplatz am Waldbad (///rational.portable.stocks). It was about seven miles outside Hamelin, the city famously cleared of rats and children by the Pied Piper in the Grimm's Fairy Tale.

Preflight Checks

Next morning, we were all set to head for rat central, but first needed to complete our pre-flight checks. Less than a week into our trip, we'd already developed a rather silly routine that we made ourselves carry out before we moved off a campsite. It involved working through a checklist in wartime RAF fighter pilot accents, as if we preparing to launch a bomber.

"Garss orf?" This was the big one.

"Yes, the LPG gas tap is off." Risk of exploding on the autobahn averted.

"Cabin doors closed?"
"Oh stink, the sliding side door hasn't shut properly again." It was often a choice between a gentle close that didn't work or a big slam that threatened to make every one of Cliff's window blinds drop out.

"Hatches secure?"
"No! The rooflight in the loo is still open. I thought *you'd* closed it."

"Fridge de-rattled?"
"Done." Loose items in the fridge had been wedged together or spaced with cloths to stop infuriating rattles.

"Umbilical cord?"
"Check." This meant the electric hook-up cable had been detached, wound up and stuffed in the cellar under the bed.

"Chocs away?"
"Affirmative". We weren't going to drive off the levelling chocs or leave them behind. They were back in their carry bag and stashed away.

In just over a year on the road, we never grew out of this farcical routine. But it did prevent some potentially costly mishaps on more occasions than you'd imagine. With everything stowed and battened down, we were ready for take-off. We taxied out of the campsite and flew off towards Hamelin and our first encounter with a Stellplatz.

Our First Stellplatz

We knew Germany was famous for its "Whonmobilstellplatz". Rough translation: "mobile home places". They're essentially parking lots where campers and motorhomes are welcome to stay the night. Many provide fresh water and facilities to dispose of dirty (grey) water or toilet (black) waste. Some even offer electric hook-ups.

French 'aires' are often held up as the gold standard of such facilities, but many other camper-friendly nations in Europe provide their own versions. They're either free or charge modest fees – making them a popular alternative to conventional campsites.

We were still building up our confidence for an overnight stay, so settled for day parking at the Hamelin Stellplatz, just to dip our toes in the water.

The site (/// wanted.rail.sanded) was easy to find. Surrounding roads had campervan signs pointing us in the right direction. First impressions? It was a car park with larger than average parking spaces. It was in an industrial area, close to some railway sidings on the outskirts of town - not the prettiest place to stay. We pulled into a parking slot and were greeted by a couple of veteran British campervanners who had spotted our UK number plate.

They told us they'd explored every inch of Europe since they bought their van in 2010. They'd always stayed in Stellplatz, or their equivalent, because they were such excellent value. They claimed they'd only had to resort to campsites five times in twelve years of European adventuring.

Maybe it was time we grew some and stopped being so apprehensive about staying overnight in a glorified car park. Soon maybe. For now, we paid €4 for four hours' parking and followed a riverside path from the Stellplatz into the heart of the rat-infested city.

Following The Piper

Hamelinners make the most of their connection with the Grimms Fairy Tale. There are giant gold rats on top of bridges, stuffed toy rats in almost every shop window and metal rat emblems buried among the cobbles which mark an official Pied Piper trail.

The historic city centre is small, with picturesque timber-framed buildings and a museum. There's also a smart modern shopping centre if you fancy a spot of rat-tail therapy. (Sorry).

Not to be missed is the famous ratcatcher story being re-enacted by an automaton Pied Piper and a horde of mechanical rats and children. The strangely mesmerising display takes place three times a day, half-way up the side of the 17th century Hochzeithaus, or Wedding House, in Hamelin's market square (///: reach.magnets.useage).

You know something's about to happen when thirty-seven bells attached to the side of the building ring out like a giant glockenspiel. A pair of bronze doors then swing open to reveal a parade of mechanical figures. The city wasn't busy when we visited, but a crowd appeared from nowhere as the display got underway. Kids of all ages loved it. Including us.

Autobahns

After collecting Cliff from the Stellplatz, we left Hamelin and rejoined the autobahn. Throughout our travels, we relied heavily on 'Shaughness' – the electronic Irishman whose dulcet tones we'd selected as the voice of our sat nav. He is so clever. He remembers details of every road in Europe and is usually a dependable guide to anywhere. But as we started following the signs towards Hamburg, we thought Shaughness was faulty.

Normally, his display of the prevailing speed limit was as valuable as his directions. It's hard to remember each country's speed limit rules and easy to miss road signs when you're focusing so hard on not getting lost.

We felt very vulnerable when the speed limit disappeared from the sat nav screen. Explanation? We were on a section of autobahn that had no speed limit to stick to.

On these extremely fast roads, we tended to hug the right hand (slow) lane, invariably finding ourselves in a never-ending convoy of trucks heading for Poland. With 140 horses under his bonnet, Cliff wasn't slow - unless we selected 'eco' mode on the auto gearbox. This fuel-saving mode left him with all the firepower of a Citroen 2CV. Even in perfectly adequate 'normal' mode, we felt safer keeping away from the plethora of Porsches and Audis that rocketed down the fast lane in a blur.

Eventually, we arrived at The Stover Strand Campsite near Drage, about forty minutes south of Hamburg (///hairdresser.turnout.appeal). It's a large holiday park beside the mighty river Elbe. After we checked in, a smiley youth on a golf buggy escorted us to our pitch only a stone's throw from a small beach on the riverbank. We spent much of the evening trying to work out how to get into Hamburg. We weren't keen on parking Cliff in Germany's second largest city.

The train and bus services we found would have taken forever. So, we decided to risk driving after all, and park at a Stellplatz in the city's tourist quarter. A place where you may also park for the night.

Happening Hamburg

Next morning, Shaughness guided us expertly through the bustling city. After some difficulty finding the entrance to the parking area, we paid €14 to a rather grumpy attendant and, to our surprise, parked next to a Russian U-boat.

U-Boat 434 is a Soviet spy sub, built in the 1970s. Now docked in the harbour near Hamburg's old fish market, it's the centrepiece of the city's U-Boat Museum (///voters.prompt.smug). This slightly sinister Tango-class sub is still operational, though its days of skulking around for Russian intelligence are long gone. You can book guided tours if you're into Soviet military hardware or claustrophobia.

The Hamburg waterfront was buzzing. Buskers performed outside cafés and bars. Families crammed onto floating seafood restaurants moored to the dockside. There was a very youthful energy about the whole harbour area.

Our first destination was the stunning, riverside concert hall, The Elbphilarmonie. Before our trip, I would not have listed architecture as one of my special interests, but wherever we went in Europe we couldn't fail to be impressed by big, bold, and daringly different buildings.

Hamburg's 'Elbi' cost a staggering €866 million. Its development was mired in controversy. Arguments between the city and architects ended up in the European court. But the result is truly spectacular. The upper part of the building resembles a giant iceberg made of glass, or an Alpine range created from crystal. It teeters on top of a more conventional brick-built base – a dockside warehouse from the 1960s.

You can take tours around the interior, but we had another architectural wonder on our hitlist. A hole in the ground.

The Elbe Tunnel

The Elbe Tunnel is a surprisingly beautiful, 426 m (1400 ft) pedestrian tunnel which goes under the Elbe riverbed. It links central Hamburg with the docks and shipyards on the river's south bank. It was opened in 1911 for the rather mundane purpose of enabling dockworkers to cross the river to work. But there's nothing mundane about the tunnel itself. It's an Art Deco-style masterpiece; a protected monument that's often used as a film set. If you're into Art Deco, hefty civil engineering or decorated ceramic tiles, you'll love it.

We stepped inside a giant cage lift at the city end of the tunnel (///rail.kite.sourced) and descended 24 m (80 ft) below ground. The tunnel itself was dry, light and surprisingly airy. We walked under the river and, on the opposite bank, took a second antiquated lift to the surface. The view back over the river towards the city was spectacular.

We enjoyed something of a flying visit to Hamburg, but it's certainly somewhere we'd return to for a long weekend.

Toilet Tech

After our second night at Stover Strand, we discovered our campsite was equipped with a rather exciting piece of equipment. A fully automated machine for emptying campervan toilet cassettes.

I promised honesty in this book and must come clean. Disposing of toilet waste is the most unpleasant aspect of campervanning. I do appreciate that our onboard loo was a godsend. It allowed us to overnight in the most incredible off-grid locations during our trip. But the inevitable process of emptying your onboard loo tank every two or three days (depending on factors too unpleasant to discuss) is gross. It was gross when we first did it. It's still gross now.

Usually, you remove your cassette from the van and trundle off to a designated dumping ground. They're often called chemical or Elsan toilets. We prefer the more descriptive name used at the first Dutch campsite we'd stayed at – loosplats! I sometimes wonder if I dreamt this, but I do have photographic evidence of the loosplats sign.

Anyhow, this German campsite had no need for loosplats or any other form of manual toilet emptying facilities. For the royal sum of €2, a machine would carry out the disgusting process for you.

It looked like a giant vending machine. Once I inserted my coins, a roller shutter opened as if by magic, inviting me to slip our full cassette inside. When the cassette was firmly in place, the roller door closed slowly. For some reason, it reminded me of a crematorium.

After the door had clicked shut, there was a great deal of whirring and swooshing. Out of view (mercifully), our cassette was being opened, emptied, and cleaned. The machine then kindly put a drop of water and waste-degrading chemicals into the plastic box.

Eventually, the shutter rolled open triumphantly. I slid the clean box out and carried it back to the van. Job done without any risk of deadly blowback or spillages.

For me, it was worth spending about £1.80. Those with stronger stomachs may disagree. We didn't see many of these auto washers on our travels, but one other – also in Germany – played a video while it did the business. At one point the video asked if I was a vegetarian, which I found profoundly disturbing.

Ready For Rostock

That evening, we needed to be close to the Baltic ferry port of Rostock. Our check in for the ferry to Sweden was at 6.30 the following morning.

As we turned up at the Baltic Freizeit site, we weren't sure what to expect. (///constitutes.retailers.slogged). From its website, we couldn't work out whether it was a campsite or a Stellpatz. It turned out to be both. There's a large campsite, mostly under the cover of a dense forest. It has great facilities including shops and a pizza restaurant. However, there's also a simple, overnight camping lot close to the entrance – ideal for the early getaway we needed.

As lazy Englanders, we'd had no problems with language barriers before this point on our travels, mostly because everyone we'd encountered in Holland and Germany spoke slightly better English than we did. Here, however, the sole guy on reception was not an English speaker. Not for the first time, we were saved by technology.

The receptionist was happy to use Google translate on Steve's phone. He explained that we didn't pay anything up front but needed €10 in coins to slot in the exit barrier when we departed. At least, that's what we thought he said. We settled down for the night, slightly nervous that catching our ferry depended on that barrier accepting our loose change.

4. HOW SWEDISH ARE WE!

Our phone alarms went off in unison at 5.45 am. We were *not* going to miss the ferry from Rostock across the Baltic Sea to Trelleborg on the south-western tip of Sweden.

The port was a twenty-minute drive from our camping spot; or it should have been. Some bright sparks chose that morning to close a main road outside the ferry terminal and we couldn't find the entrance. After circling dockside warehouses and stacks of shipping containers several times, stress levels rose to eye-popping levels. A shortage of signs in English didn't help. We finally joined the queue at passport control with four minutes to spare (///charcoal.shout.back).

We'd pre-booked the six-hour voyage online for £153. Top Tip: Don't miss the sausage-shaped Swedish meatballs if you sail this route.

Taking The Plunge

After an uneventful voyage, we drove off the ferry onto Swedish soil, cleared border control with ease and headed north-east. Our first destination was Orebackens Camping, an immaculate forest campsite close to the town of Sjöbo (///cartoonist.soothingly.flute). It was everything we expected from Scandinavia. It was pristine and well-ordered, with neat pitches well spaced-out under mature pine trees. The air tasted Scandi fresh.

The next morning, we discovered our campsite fee included two tickets to a giant, open air swimming pool close by. How Swedish was that! Neither of us are natural-born water babies, but *this* opportunity warranted a rummage through Cliff's deep storage for our swim shorts.

Friendly William at the campsite reception assured us that the Olympic-size pool was a cosy twenty-seven degrees. I didn't believe him. My scepticism was probably rooted in childhood trauma - deeply suppressed memories of my one and only dip in the icy waters of the open-air pool on Whitby's clifftop.

However, William was spot on. This pristine pool was unbelievably warm. It was spotlessly clean and in a stunning setting half-way down the wooded hill between our campsite and the nearby town. We enjoyed swimming a few lengths, dried in the mid-July sun, then made our way back to the van to prepare for the epic journey to our next stopover - all of twenty minutes away.

We'd spotted an opportunity to dip our toes into so-called 'wild camping' - something we really needed to master before we headed off-grid in Sweden's northern wilderness.

The Swedish Right To Roam.

Sweden has an extremely healthy approach to its vast countryside. It starts from the premise that the wilderness belongs to everyone, so gives its citizens and visitors a legal 'right to roam'. I appreciate this is hard to believe if you've grown up in England where the basic approach is more along the lines of "Keep Out", "No Camping" or "Trespassers will be shot".

Strictly speaking, Scandinavia's right to roam laws are for walkers and tentists, not people travelling and sleeping in motor vehicles. But the general positivity about accessing the countryside rubs off for those of us in campervans and motorhomes. There's a general acceptance that you can park overnight in remote locations, providing you follow a basic code of behaviour. There's a detailed country-by-country guide to wild camping laws in many European countries in my previous book *Europe by Campervan*.

Going Off The Grid (A Little)

We chose to test our new-found camping freedom in a public car park that serves the vast Snogeholm Recreation area (/// tuition.navigable.telescopic). This unspoilt area of woodland contains three large lakes. It's a mecca for hikers, cyclists, canoeists, horse riders and folk who fish. But its car park has no facilities for camping. We would have to be self-sufficient, relying on our tank of fresh water, our onboard loo and leisure battery topped up by our solar panel. I know a car park isn't really going off-grid, but we had to start somewhere.

That afternoon, we were exploring the shores of nearby Lake Snogeholmssjön when we came across a stack of kayaks for hire. There was a locked shed close by, but no sign of any lifeforms. The absence of humans would become a recurring theme throughout our Scandinavian adventures. In these sparsely populated countries, it often felt that we had the countryside to ourselves.

Hiring the kayaks involved a web-based booking system and a degree of trust we couldn't imagine working in the UK. First, we went online and selected our four-hour slot. We paid via the website and a few minutes before our session was due to start, we were texted a security code for the lock on the afore-mentioned shed's door. Once inside the hut, we helped ourselves to life jackets and paddles, locked the shed behind us and launched our kayak from a small jetty. That simple.

We spent a very enjoyable couple of hours watching cows paddling at the lake's edge, circling islands, bobbing around beds of yellow water lilies, and watching dragonflies make babies. When we'd had enough, we put the kayak and its accessories back where we had found them - just as we'd been trusted to do.

That night, despite having made the slightly alarming discovery that Swedish forests have bears (not many I hasten to add), we had a perfectly decent night's sleep. Our first tentative step at wild camping was a success and made even sweeter by not costing a Krona.

A Stairway To Heaven

With renewed confidence, we headed north, vaguely in the direction of Stockholm. We were in no hurry and planned to investigate whatever caught our attention en route. Our first unexpected discovery was a sculpture park just south of Kivik (///gripped.affiliates.farmed).

Back home, we're big fans of our local sculpture park near Wakefield, West Yorkshire. This does not mean we are art experts. Far from it. Official explanations of what modern art represents make no sense to me whatsoever. However, we are both keen photographers and fully aware that slightly bonkers objects in the landscape provide great photo opportunities. So, when Steve found the Kivik Art Centre online, we had to take a look.

Even the official blurb about Kivik concedes it's difficult to define. I'd say it was an area of wooded hillside, dotted with art installations and sculptures that mess up your head. It's more puzzling than pretentious. Awe-inspiring as well as amusing.

After parking Cliff in the car park (a field), we set off on a circular trail through the woodland. We encountered "The Stairway to Heaven" – an apparently unsupported staircase stretching 18m (60ft) into the sky. In a clearing, there was a 1970s plastic cottage in Chopper bike orange, once hailed as a solution to a Scandinavian housing crisis. Close by, what looked like a full-sized chicken shed was rotating on a huge spit.

We climbed a pitch-dark stairwell inside one giant concrete structure, emerging at treetop level on a platform that had no handrails.

If you're a health and safety expert, maybe give that one a miss. I can't claim to have understood anything we saw at Kivik, but our visit was great fun and generated some great photos. Check them out on Steve's Instagram page: https://www.instagram.com/cheerfulheartphotography/

Flat-Pack Fantastic

While Kivik had been a chance discovery, our next encounter with Scandinavian design was deliberate. We were determined to call at IKEA. Not a local store, but the official IKEA Museum in Älmhult, the town where the now ubiquitous flat-pack furniture makers opened their first store in 1958.

The night before our visit, we stayed ten minutes away from the museum at First Camp Sjöstugan (///invoke.shrugging.caffeine), a busy, family campsite on a beautiful lakeside. But when we arrived at the museum the next morning, we found we could have overnighted in its car park for free. Several campers had clearly been there all night.

The IKEA Museum and many of its stores throughout Sweden and Norway, encourage overnight parking in their car parks. They don't provide camping facilities, just well-lit, designated camper spaces. Of course, there's the bonus of being able to visit a store's restaurant and toilets during opening hours. We made a mental note to sample IKEA's hospitality in future and headed into the ultra-modern looking museum (///instincts.tuesdays.unhelpful).

I've been genuinely surprised how many our friends have had difficulty believing that a) an IKEA museum exists and b), we enjoyed it so much.

The museum works on many levels. First, it tells the story behind a brand that's so familiar we never stop to think about it. It's strangely nostalgic, displaying the stuff of everyday life that was once so mundane and familiar, we hadn't realised we'd forgotten about it.

The exhibits are also about design; an insight into the clever and detailed thinking behind household items like lamps, bookcases, sofas, and kitchen utensils that we take for granted. The brand is up front about its failures as well as its successes in trying to mass produce 'designer' items at the lowest possible prices.

It's also a fascinating one-man business story. Ingvar Kamprad started selling matches at the age of five and founded IKEA when he was just seventeen. Incidentally, "IKEA" comes from Ingvar Kamprad's initials… I.K; plus the E from Elmtaryd, the farm he grew up on; and the A from Agunnaryd, his nearby village. That's one pub quiz question nailed.

Kamprad played a pivotal role in growing his company into the world's biggest home furnishing retailer with stores in forty-nine countries.

The museum also celebrates the iconic IKEA catalogue; the only welcome form of junk mail I can think of. It dropped through letterboxes for over seventy years. There are displays of iconic front covers and the chance to appear on one. We posed on a photoshoot set, smiled at the automated camera, and got a free print-out of us on a front cover to take home.

And did we finish off our visit with meatballs in the museum restaurant? Of course we did.

5. ISLAND HOPPING AND DISCOVERING STOCKHOLM

Sweden has 221,800 islands and our next destination was one of them. We headed north from Älmhult, up the E4 highway for about three hours, to a small ferry terminal in Gränna near the southern end of Lake Vättern (///sustain.qualifying.maintaining). We joined a queue of cars, bikes, campers, and pedestrians waiting for one of two yellow car ferries to shuttle us across to Visingsö Island.

This may be a bit sad, but I find small ferries quite exciting. It must be because we hardly ever see them in the UK. In Scandinavia, with so many lakes, fjords, and vast sea inlets to cross, ferries are a key element of the transport system. Some crossings form part of road routes because there's no asphalt alternative.

We'd been good boys and booked our £24 return ticket online, as recommended on the ferry operator's website. When our boat came in, we drove Cliff onto the open car deck.

At 83 miles long (135 km), Vättern is the second biggest lake in Sweden. According to legend, the island that's half-way across it was created by a giant. He scooped up a handful of earth and threw it into the lake so his mother could use it as a stepping stone. That makes sense.

After a 25-minute voyage, we drove off the ferry and found our campsite close to the terminal (///positions.reaction.elbows). We had pre-booked a £22 per night pitch because the island can be busy in summer.

Visingsö Island

Visingsö Island is almost nine miles (14 km) long and two miles (3 km) wide. About 750 people live there full-time, but it's chiefly a tourist destination. Island activities include kayaking, boat cruises and fishing. You can take a hike or a horse-drawn carriage through oak forests. The northern end of the island is great for birdwatching. While the island's roads are wide enough for vehicles, we opted to explore on hired bicycles - £13 each for three hours.

We made the most of the peace and tranquillity of island life because our next destination was the big city.

Stockholm Sights

Three weeks into our grand tour, Cliff had already transported us to some amazing locations. But cities weren't his natural habitat - especially capitals the size of Stockholm. So, we set about finding somewhere to stay on the outskirts and rely on public transport for our urban exploring.

It was the third week in July, and several of the campsites we tried were fully booked - a downside of not planning your overnights far enough in advance.

Bredang Camping, six miles (10 km) south-west of Stockholm had no vacancies, but a friendly chap on the phone suggested we should turn up early the next day as spaces usually became available. Luckily, our gamble paid off.

Bredang (///reminder.beard.flame) was the busiest place we'd been to in three weeks and the site felt a little overcrowded. However, the facilities were good. We made use of the laundry and enjoyed a walk down to the nearby lake where families were swimming and diving from jetties and pontoons.

For us, the best thing about the site was its location – a short walk from the Bredang metro stop. The next day, we headed for the station, bought 72-hour travel passes (£24 each) and hopped on line 13 to Stockholm central station.

Stockholm's attractive old town offered the familiar tourist mix of restaurants, designer boutiques and souvenir shops. Changing the guard at The Royal Palace amused us (///dressing.responds.petty). The ritualistic handover of duties from one guard to another involved a rather elaborate and slightly camp dance. It looked somewhat at odds with the serious business of protecting the Swedish monarchy. I apologise for our disrespectful tittering, though I guess non-Brits have a good snigger at our ancient ceremonies too.

A Feast Of Photos

We walked through the city and along the harbourside to Fotografiska, a museum of contemporary photography housed in the old Customs House in Stockholm harbour (///fairly.tracking.sweat). We hit on an amazing exhibition of photos by the late Terry O'Neill, famous for the striking images of the fashions, pop stars and royals he snapped during the 1960s. It will have moved on now because the museum has fifteen to twenty different exhibitions each year, but don't miss it if you spot it elsewhere. We had an amazing afternoon in the company of David Bowie, Elton John, The Beatles, Rolling Stones, Kate Moss, and Queen Elizabeth II.

The museum's smart, top-floor café has spectacular views over

Stockholm's vast harbour, including Gröna Lund, Sweden's oldest amusement park across the water on Djurgården Island (///strapped.limp.renews). The 140-year-old attraction has eight roller coasters and other seriously stomach-churning rides. You can grab a water taxi from Fotografiska to the theme park if you feel the need.

Meatball Maestros

We were hungry, and headed to Stockholm's nearby hipster district, *Södermalm,* in search of food. Among the cool barbers, galleries and vintage clothes shops we found "Meatballs for the People" – a small restaurant which, unsurprisingly, specialised in Swedish meatballs (///talkers.bicker.hops).

Delicacies on the menu included meatballs made from bear, boar, reindeer, and moose. We took the line of least resistance and went for the chef's choice of four flavours. Chef must have been having an unadventurous day because we got beef, venison, pork, and chicken. They were nonetheless delicious and served with mashed potatoes, creamy veal gravy, preserved lingonberries and pickled cucumber. With a small lager each, our bill came to about £53.

The next day, we returned to central Stockholm on the metro and headed for the attractions on *Djurgården* – one of the fourteen islands that make up the capital city.

We walked past the popular Viking Museum (///dared.jazzy.floating) as we expected to have our fill of Norsemen when we reached Norway. Instead, just around the corner, we learned about another bunch of world-conquering Swedes at The ABBA Museum (///arrival.reach.hands).

Abba Museum

I trust you're aware that it's now officially cool to adore ABBA. I always have. It's to do with my age. Not long before we left Blighty, Steve, our ABBAmaniac friends and I saw the truly astonishing holographic, virtual, blimey what is actually happening here ABBA Voyage concert in London. It was without doubt the best concert experience I've had – even though I'm still not 100% sure what I witnessed. It left me keen to see how the official ABBA museum in the Super Troopers' own country would tell their amazing story.

The museum does an excellent job charting the group's rise to world domination with interviews, concert footage and artefacts. It's packed with the band's stage clothes and instruments. You can even try audio mixing ABBA's early hits in a recreated recording studio. I managed to ruin Voulez Vous. And while it's way more fun and has more hands-on interactivity than many museums, it wasn't quite as amazing as I'd expected.

Worryingly, it's now half a century since "Waterloo" (ABBA's Eurovision-winning song, not the battle). The group are still *so* popular, you can watch their story on repeat in countless TV documentaries. Perhaps that's why some of the film and TV clips in the museum felt a bit familiar. True ABBA fans will love it, but I'm not sure they will discover anything new.

I reckon my teeniest bit of disappointment was simply because I was still reeling from sheer, ground-breaking brilliance, and hi-tech wizardry of ABBA Voyage.

Underground Art

In most capitals, travelling by underground can be grim. Stockholm's metro system is the exception. At 68 miles (110 km), it's officially the longest art gallery in the world. Most stations have a few, modest arty features, but some are complete art installations in themselves.

Artists have transformed vast, hollowed-out caverns and tunnels, painting the bare rock. Some stations are a riot of colour from their platforms to the ceilings of their escalator halls. There are murals, models, and mosaics; dioramas sunk into the walls; statues loitering by the ticket machines.

Travel passes and cameras in hand, we rode the red and blue lines, hopping off at the most spectacular metro art stops. A good starting point is T-Centralen station (///risks.compounds.stylist). From there, you can visit Stadion and Tekniska Högskolan stations on the red line and hop over to Solna Centrum, Tensta, Kungsträdgården and Rådhuset on the blue line.

We spent a couple of hours underground on a weekday afternoon in mid-July and the stations weren't too busy. The whole experience costs no more than your metro ticket. The underground art gallery is also a useful refuge should Stockholm turn wet or cold above ground. After our final art-station stop off, we stayed on the metro until it delivered us back to Bredang – that short walk from our campsite.

6. WILDERNESS CAMPING AND A PLAGUE OF FROGS

After making the most of civilisation, it was time to tackle our first truly wild camping. But before we headed north into the Swedish wilderness, we needed to increase our chances of survival by topping up on the LPG gas that fuelled our heating and cooking.

What A Gas

We discovered, before we left home, that the gas cannister swapsies system campervanners use in the UK doesn't really work in the rest of Europe. European countries either have unique systems with their own bottle sizes and connectors; operate several systems that are incompatible with UK bottles and each other (France); or don't do swapsies at all.

The solution, we were told, was to fit re-fillable gas bottles in the van which could be topped up with LPG at service stations throughout Europe. We went for twin bottles. It cost us about £750, including fitting and a set of European adapters.

Overall, it was a lifesaver. But in a handful of places, we still struggled to find LPG refill points. Surprisingly, the outskirts of Stockholm were one of them. We ended up driving an hour out of our way to one LPG point that came up on our gas-finding app. It wasn't a service station; it was a gas specialist on an industrial estate. The man running it seemed a little surprised when we turned up, but obligingly topped up our gas tanks from a weird contraption inside his shed.

"How much do we owe you?"

No reply. The man just held out his card machine displaying the total in Krona. We hadn't got our heads around the exchange rate at that point, but our bank app told us we'd filled two tanks for £5.62. Bargain. We'd spent more in diesel getting there. Top Tip: if you see an LPG pump, top up. You never know when you'll see another one.

Into The Wilderness

With enough gas on board to explore the Arctic, we headed back north, skirted around Stockholm, headed towards Upsala on the E4, then off the motorways, north-west, on the 272.

The landscape was beginning to look more like what we'd expected from Scandinavia. More forests, more lakes - attractive little farming communities dotted with red painted barns. The rural roads were far better than we'd imagined - and quieter too.

After driving for more than three hours, our agreed daily maximum, we started searching for our first real off-grid overnight site in the forest – i.e., not an official car park. After a certain amount of dithering, we finally chose a spot beside a rough forest track just north of Ockelbo (///bitter.affirmation.habitat).

Eventually, we would become seasoned off-gridders. But on that first night, we were paranoid. The "right to roam" code said we must not camp near dwellings. We spotted some boarded-up forest cabins further down the track, but after some debate decided they were far enough away. We'd seen a sign for the Trollberget Nature Reserve but had no idea if we were actually in it. Camping in reserves is not allowed. Checks on Google Maps didn't really clarify anything, so we made a joint assumption that we were legal.

It was getting dark by the time we battened down the hatches and applied the bear straps. I mentioned earlier that wild bears roam the Swedish forests. Just under three thousand of them at the last count. We were taking no chances.

Steve's seasoned campervanning friend Sarah had scared us witless before we embarked on our trip. She told us how she'd been sleeping in her van in a designated rest stop, and someone had broken in. Since then, she'd always tied her driver and passenger doors together with strong webbing straps. We'd bought a set online for about a tenner and, on finding out about Sweden's large hairy wildlife situation, christened them the bear straps.

We both knew that the effectiveness of this rather unnecessary layer of extra protection depended entirely on any marauding bears choosing to use the van's front doors, rather than the double doors at the back or the sliding side door. Nonetheless, on our first night sleeping in the forest, we pulled the buckles on the straps tight.

We had a surprisingly restful and bear-free night and woke to a silent, slightly misty morning in the forest. I stepped outside to grab some photos of Cliff in his first wilderness location. Wading through the undergrowth to get a good shot, I discovered the ground was covered with wild berries. Loads of them.

The Swedish 'right to roam' also allows you to forage. Landowners can't stop you gathering the fruits of the forest, providing you intend to eat them yourself and you don't cut down bushes or break twigs or branches while collecting them.

I was surprised to see wild raspberries. Smaller than the garden varieties, they're common throughout the Swedish countryside. A quick internet check identified Swedish blueberries – for jam-making apparently - and dark red lingonberries, commonly turned into the saucy condiment which accompanies any self-respecting portion of

Swedish meatballs. I resisted the temptation to forage, as we weren't exactly equipped for jam or condiment production.

A Plague Of Frogs

Having established ourselves as campervanning's answers to Bear Grylls, we headed further north. After another stunning, three-hour drive, we came to what became one of my favourite overnight locations on our entire Scandinavian trip.

Steve discovered Naturrastplats Ljusnanfluss (a nature rest area) near Alby on a motorhome and campervan app, as he did most of our great stopovers throughout Europe (///saltwater.imbued.fleshy).

Our favourite and most-used app is "Park4Night". Just download the free version to your phone and try it out. We stepped up to the paid-for version (€2.49 per month or €9.99 for the year) because it has extra features. The dated reviews left by previous visitors to locations were an enormous influence on where we stayed.

We also used the Campercontact app which recommended the beautiful riverside rest area we arrived at that afternoon. A rough forest track led from the main road down to the water's edge before following the shoreline. There were spaces for about a dozen campers along the bank in gaps between trees. We wiggled Cliff into one of them and opened the sliding side door. What a room with a view!

The river was so still and wide it looked like a giant mirror, reflecting the million greens of the tree-covered hillside on the opposite bank. The only sound was water cascading over a weir a short distance downstream. Idyllic. (See main chapter photo).

There were no facilities, other than an extremely unpleasant toilet in a solitary hut. Everything else about the location was stunning.

We explored upstream, scrambling through woodland carpeted with thick moss. A Swedish woman from a nearby motorhome was fishing by a small waterfall. She agreed it was a beautiful location, but warned we should look out for vipers that like to loiter at the water's edge.

The common European viper (or adder as we know them back home) is slightly venomous. Each year, about four hundred Swedes end up in hospital having been bitten by one of these sneaky snakes. Only a third of patients have moderate to severe symptoms and fatalities are extremely rare. I'm still not entirely sure what possessed us, but this information didn't stop us taking a dip in the river before tea.

Early next morning, we were woken by a spectacular downpour. Raindrops clattered on the roof of the van. The river was a cauldron of bubbles and splashes. It wasn't the best weather for camping, but it was perfect for frogs - hundreds of them.

When the storm passed, we stepped out of the van into a plague of froglets. The cute little amphibians, no bigger than a thumbnail, were on the move. The saturated ground was covered with them as they made their way from the forest behind us towards the river. There were so many, we stayed inside the van for fear of squashing them. After an hour, the froggy phenomena was over and after doing our now familiar pre-flight checks, we moved on.

7. THE SWEDISH HIGH COAST

By now, we'd clocked up about two thousand miles on our Nordic adventure and our next destination was the unique landscape of Sweden's High Coast.

We made a brief, lunchtime stop-off in town of Härnösand. It had an attractive riverside (///copycat.mugs.legal), a shopping centre and a motor museum - but hardly any sign of life. Half-way up Sweden, we were getting the distinct feeling hardly anyone lived there.

We decided to move on and soon crossed the impressive High Coast Bridge (Högakustenbron). It's the gateway to the High Coast region and at 1,867 m (6,125 ft), the fourth longest suspension bridge in Europe.

It's striking enough from the passenger seat of a campervan, but even more spectacular when viewed from the large rest area at the northern end of the bridge (///limousines.rebuild.zinc). (See picture above). The rest stop has designated parking for campers, where overnights are allowed. There are toilets, a restaurant and a hotel. We'd only been travelling for a short time so pressed on into High Coast country.

The Swedish High Coast is tricky to describe. In the UK, we're accustomed to the coast being a fairly defined line where the land meets the sea. The Swedish High Coast is more a disorientating patchwork of islands, sea inlets and lakes.

It boasts the highest coastline in the world at approximately 286 m (938 ft) above sea level. But the unique feature of the landscape is that it's rising by about 8mm (a third of an inch) every year. During the last ice age, the whole area was crushed under the weight of a two-mile (3 km) thick layer of ice. Since the ice melted 9,600 years ago, the land has been slowly re-emerging out of the sea. "Glacial rebound" is its proper name.

The result is a dramatic landscape with large areas of wilderness, red granite rocks, lakes and islands. It's a top destination for hikers, kayakers and off-road adventurists. After a spectacular though somewhat disorientating drive, we parked up at a roadside picnic area for the night (///calculation.barge.unlike).

Mannaminne Madness

It has been said that I have an over-developed sense of the ridiculous. Nowhere has it come in more useful than at the Mannaminne open air museum, one of the most visited and eccentric attractions on The High Coast (///archduke.confesses.tans).

The museum is spread over four-acres of hillside. Eclectic doesn't quite do it justice. Its exhibits range from a Swedish-built Saab Draken jet fighter to a collection of macabre marionettes. There's an accordion collection, an entire building full of ancient sleds and farming equipment; plus, army trucks, boats, deep-sea submersibles, trams, and a subway train. Parts of the site feel like a scrapyard – in a good way.

Mannaminne was the brainchild of the late Swedish artist Anders Åberg. We already knew some of his work – the decoration of the Solna Centrum metro station back in Stockholm. Here, with his wife

Barbro, he'd aimed to create a meeting place for anyone interest in arts and crafts.

The site features over fifty buildings; some built on site, others rescued from around Sweden, or other countries, and re-assembled. There's the Hungarian house, a Mexican temple and a Chinese pavilion which doubles as a café. It's like a folksy, homemade version of Disney's EPCOT Centre.

If you prefer your museums to be organised, with neat displays and lots of explanatory labels, Mannaminne will disappoint you. We had absolutely no idea what many exhibits were or why they were there. It's surprising, chaotic and we absolutely loved it.

Flat-Pack Parking

From Mannaminne, we travelled two hours up The High Coast until we reached civilisation - Umeå in northern Sweden. We pulled into the giant parking lot at the IKEA superstore on the south-western outskirts of the university town (///amends.update.claps).

I've mentioned that IKEA stores in Sweden and Norway positively encourage campers and motorhomes to overnight in their parking lots. We arrived mid-afternoon and bagged a space before having a good look around the retail park. We visited a large Willys supermarket to buy a few essentials. Willys are a common site throughout Sweden. The discount grocery chain has over 230 stores.

As night fell, it felt a little strange to be hunkering down in a shopping centre parking lot. Though we were re-assured that folks in several other campers and motorhomes were doing the same. It wasn't the prettiest location we'd stayed in, but it was free, convenient, well-lit, and felt safe.

Next morning, after a hearty breakfast in the IKEA restaurant, we hit the road and changed direction. After heading north up the Swedish coast for the last week or so, we headed inland, north-west on the E12, in the general direction of northern Norway.

The countryside was less dramatic than it had been on The High Coast. It was gentler, more agricultural, dotted with farmsteads and small villages. It was late July, and we assumed everyone would be out making the most of the pleasant weather. There was no-one to be seen. There was hardly any traffic either.

The Cut-Down Car Cult.

What we did see, and got stuck behind, were very slow-moving cars displaying red triangles. They looked as if they were broken and limping to a garage. But it turns out they would never go faster than 19 mph (30 km/h) even in perfect working order.

They're a uniquely Swedish phenomenon known as A-tractors, or EPA tractors. As a lifelong petrolhead, I couldn't believe I'd not heard of them before.

Their roots go back to World War II when Swedish farmers were short of money and tractors. Wartime rationing (rubber for tyres for example) left many sturdy old cars unfit for the road and laid up in barns. The farmers solved their tractor shortage by modifying their redundant old cars to do jobs like pulling trailers and carrying bales of hay around their farms.

Eventually, the Swedish government allowed these adapted vehicles on the roads providing they met certain rules. Stipulations included:

* A towbar to pull a 1000 kg trailer.

* No space for passengers or goods behind the driver (i.e., no second row of seats). This usually resulted in a cut-down cab.

* Some form of truck bed to carry goods.

* A speed limit of 30 km/h (i.e., tractor speed limits), usually achieved by altering the gearing.

* A warning "slow vehicle" triangle displayed on the back.

But the big news - you could drive these adapted vehicles from the age of fifteen, providing you had a moped or a tractor licence. Sweden's youth, in rural areas at least, wasted no time converting cheap old cars and started a sub-culture akin to young Americans and their hot rods.

Early Volvos were popular for conversion. And as we were about to discover, for true followers, they still are.

When we drove into the small town of Lycksele, we could not believe our eyes. It was packed. There were cars parked nose-to-tail on every verge. Makeshift car parks were overflowing. The pavements were crammed with people heading towards a lake. The roads were jammed with vintage American cars and every variation of converted, pimped-up A-tractor you could imagine. It looked as though every car fan in Sweden was in town (///sigh.toolbar.tiptoes).

We had accidentally hit on two major events – the annual, nine-day Motorveckan 1950s music and car show, and an international jet ski competition. We parked Cliff in a field and battled our way through the chaos. I've no idea where rural Swedes hide most of the time, but when they come out to party, they party.

After soaking up the carnival atmosphere and taking far too many photos of beautifully restored American old-timers, we returned to the van, grabbed a quick lunch, and continued our journey north-west.

Snow Chains And Mosquitos

After Lycksele, the Swedish countryside became even more remote. The road was still in excellent condition, but pretty much deserted. Snow chain signs appeared at the bottom of hills – a warning of how inhospitable this area would be in winter. We didn't have any snow chains on board at that point. That would become a drama much later in our adventure.

We passed miles of cultivated forests. So much forest, we literally couldn't see the view for the trees. There were stages where it felt very claustrophobic. Having driven for nearly four hours that day, we started looking for somewhere to stay the night.

We checked out a couple of clearings in forests but ruled them out because they were already occupied – by mosquitos. For nearly a month on the road, we'd managed to avoid any serious encounters with the evil bloodsuckers. But there, in dense forest, presumably near water which they love, dreaded mozzies were everywhere. (Fear not. The photo is of a model mozzie at the Mannaminne Musuem!)

It was getting late when we rolled into our third choice of location, a small track between the road and a river just south of Slagnäs. The flying demons were waiting for us there too. But it was getting late, so we decided to risk it (///pods.valves.broadcasts).

I wish I could share top tips on keeping mozzies out of your camper and recommend a repellent that's guaranteed to keep them at bay. But I have none. Nothing seems to work. We battened down all our hatches, sprayed ourselves with powerful chemicals and hardly ventured outside the van. Yet still the evil bar stewards managed to attack and leave us with bites that itched for nearly three weeks.

Generally, mosquitos weren't as bad as we'd expected, considering we were in Scandinavia from mid to late summer. Mostly, we were lucky to find mozzie free locations. But that night near Slagnäs was a bad one.

8. SPECTACULAR NORWAY AND THE MIDNIGHT SUN

Next day, we emerged from our cloud of mozzies and continued our drive towards the top of Sweden. We were 2,500 miles (4000 km) into our grand tour and, if I'm being totally honest, on this day, felt ever so slightly bored. All we could see from the van was trees. An occasional lake broke the endless forest, but then there was another hundred miles of trees.

I can't tell you how excited I was when the monotony was broken by a young elk, standing on the wide verge between the road and… the trees. We drove past the cute little creature, stopped, and I jumped out of the van clutching my camera.

I'm rather fascinated by elk. (Stick with me here.) Years ago, I made a TV programme on this history of the Saab car brand. I remember a company engineer explaining that Saabs were made extra strong to withstand an impact from elk.

Elk are a member of the deer family and often confused with moose. They live in Sweden's dense forests, where for much of the year it's misty and dark. They can weigh up to a tonne. Their hefty bodies are at windscreen height, perched on rather spindly legs. If you accidentally run into one in your car, they may smash through the windscreen and land in your lap.

So, good old Saabs had strengthened A-pillars to support the windscreen. This helped flip any elk you might wallop safely over your roof. Safe for *you* that is - not for the elk. Saab even designed its own "elk test", driving new car models into a dummy elk at speed.

It's a significant issue. About 60,000 wildlife accidents happen on Swedish roads each year. Most personal injuries are the result of collisions with elk, and you'll see elk warning signs beside many roads. Swedish drivers fit extra spotlights to their cars to help spot these slightly gormless looking creatures when driving in poor conditions.

Anyhow. Our elk was only a baby. I got some great photos and video as it crossed the road, grazed for a while, wandered past Cliff, and eventually sauntered off into the forest. It was only after I'd triumphantly posted a video of my first elk encounter on Facebook that I discovered, online, that it wasn't an elk at all. It was a baby reindeer. Exciting enough, but not the four-legged forest dweller I'd been craving to see.

Despite all the road sign warnings and the thousands of miles we travelled in Scandinavia, the only elk I saw was a stuffed one in a souvenir shop. Gutted.

That night, we had a good sleep in a mosquito-free spot on a section of disused road. We needed a good rest. The next day would see us in three countries.

A Flying Visit To Finland

It was around this time that we ditched our vague plan to visit Nordkap, the northern most point of Norway. We had just about overdosed on trees and feared travelling to the extreme north would involve enduring yet more days of the same. So, we decided the Norwegian city of Tromsø would be our northern limit. The issue was how to get there.

We were astounded at the quality of main roads in northern Sweden – especially considering the extreme weather they're subjected to in winter. But they're rather scarce in the northern territories, and as a result, it's hard to find very direct routes from A to B.

Sticking to main roads, we travelled north up the E10, then took the E45 as far as it went, to Sweden's most northerly town, Karesuando, on the southern bank of the Muonio River.

We called at a service station and, while filling up with diesel, emptied our grey water waste into a conveniently placed drain. The attendant confirmed we were allowed to do this.

A sharp left turn in the town centre took us over the river, and the border into the fourth country on our adventure – Finland (/// strongest.sprain.unlocking).

We didn't do Finland justice. We tracked west along the E8 road, following the northern bank of the river, hardly losing sight of Sweden on the opposite bank. After about ninety minutes, we passed another low-key border into Norway. Country number five – and our third nation that day.

I know borders between countries are just lines on maps: their positions usually determined by political and historical upheavals. But we were convinced that whenever we crossed a border, the whole vibe and the character of the landscape changed instantly. There was no mistaking we were now in Norway. Ranges of purple-blue mountains appeared in the distance and, 2,700 miles into our trip, we had our first glimpse of snow.

Driving through one small village, we got stuck behind a hefty reindeer. I've no idea if the creature was tame or just enjoyed a stroll into town. It walked carefully along the white line in the centre of the road as if on a tightrope, holding up traffic for at least ten minutes before it veered off into a field.

Midnight Sun

We finally arrived at our overnight stop – a pebbly beach just north of the village of *Skibotn*, on the shores of the spectacular, 51 mile (82 km) long Lyngen Fjord. We parked up with our side door facing the clear water. The view across to snow-capped mountains in the distance was stunning (///smart.courtyard.blip).

Apart from another couple of campers further along the shore, we had the place to ourselves. It was one of those days we wished would never end. And actually; it didn't. We watched a film late into the evening and when we wandered down to the fjord's edge at midnight, it was still light. The Land of the Midnight Sun does what it says on the tin.

It was July 29th, and at the bewitching hour, it was light enough to see everything around us and take photos.

Knowing the sun doesn't set in parts of Northern Norway at certain times of the year is one thing; experiencing a complete lack of darkness at midnight is something else. It's weird and slightly disorientating. We thought we'd have difficulty nodding off, but Cliff's window blinds blotted out most of the midnight sun and we slept like babies.

9. TROMSØ – GATEWAY TO THE ARCTIC

Next morning, it was (still) sunny - perfect for our two-hour drive to Tromsø on the most spectacular route of our adventure so far.

We zig-zagged our way along the edges of vast fjords. Snow-capped peaks towered above us. Vast expanses of water glistened. Entire mountain ranges stretched as far as we could see. Turning every corner revealed another vista in blues, greens, and greys - all so vivid in the unfiltered Arctic light. Slightly overwhelmed by the majesty of what we'd driven through, we finally rolled into Tromsø.

The city is an outpost - a lively, civilised oasis in a harsh, inhospitable landscape of rock, ice, and water. Historically, it's been the starting point for major arctic expeditions. It's often called "The Gateway to the Arctic" or "The Paris of the North".

Most of Tromsø city is on an island which, since 1960, has been connected to the mainland by the Tromsø Bridge (/// stables.jokes.resort). This elegant structure is about two-thirds of a mile (1030 m) long and, as we discovered when we drove over it, queasily high. Spindly supports hold the centre section 38 m (124 ft) above the water, high enough for visiting cruise ships to pass underneath.

We had several must-see locations on our wish list but were up against the clock to do some shopping. Our cheap, supermarket camping chairs had collapsed from intense use, and we needed stronger replacements. The only campervan and motorhome dealership within hundreds of miles was on Tromsø island. As it was Saturday, it was due to close at lunchtime – in less than an hour.

Sat-nav Saughness directed us off the Tromsø Bridge and straight into a network of tunnels under the island city. Negotiating our first underground roundabout was a bit of a drama. We'd lost the satellite signal, so circled the subterranean junction several times, guessing which of five tunnel exits to take. Our innate sense of direction failed on this occasion. We eventually emerged from a tunnel at the wrong side of the island, so had only ten minutes to spare when we finally arrived at the campervan dealership (///roosts.conquest.daily).

With smart new camping chairs stowed in 'the cellar' (the cargo area under Cliff's fixed bed), we headed back through the city tunnels, crossed back over the bridge again and arrived at one of Tromsø's famous motifs, the Arctic Cathedral.

The Arctic Cathedral

A grand tour of Europe can leave you a little overdosed on ancient cathedrals. But the one in Tromsø is a modern, minimalist stunner. We parked behind the triangular, white building. (///galaxies.downward.range). Free parking for four hours. A great start.

The cathedral is so simple. It's constructed from rectangular, aluminium-coated concrete panels. They lean together, like giant playing cards, joining at the top to form a triangular tunnel.

Inside, floor to ceiling windows between the panels fill the interior with light. The sun shone through big, bold, stained-glass windows - splashing the plain, almost severe interior with a kaleidoscope of colours. The entrance fee was well worth £9.37 out of our daily budget.

Towering behind the Cathedral is the Tromsdalstinden mountain. At

1,238 m (4,062 ft), it dominates the landscape. In January, its peak catches the sun several days before the city below emerges from its annual spell of perpetual winter darkness.

In summer, hardy folk take day-long treks to the summit. We took the popular tourist option to a viewing platform a mere 421 m (1,400 ft) up the mountain in the Fjellheisen, the city's famous cable car.

Tromsø Panorama

The cable car's ground station is just a short walk from the cathedral (///spilling.ready.retiring). We were a little taken aback to discover ticket prices were even steeper than our up-coming ascent. The return trip (four minutes each way) cost us a total of £54.54. But it *was* worth it. (See main chapter photo).

The view from the upper cable car station was truly spectacular. We could see the whole of Tromsø; our now familiar bridge, cruise ships moored in the sound and the airport on the far side of the island. Beyond, there were mountains and fjords in all directions.

We left the crowds milling around the viewpoint and café and followed a path along the mountainside. We soon met a group of paragliders who were taking it in turn to launch themselves over the precipice. We watched these fearless individuals perform aerial acrobatics before they spiraled down to the base of the mountain, landing as a mere spec. These characters must have had day passes for the cable car because they soon re-appeared at the viewing platform, unpacked their canopies, and prepared themselves for another leap.

After taking the cable car back down the mountain, we collected Cliff and headed back over Tromsø bridge and plunged into the city's underground tunnels once again. This time, we emerged by the airport and crossed another big bridge to yet another island.

Steve's online research had discovered another great stopover location beside the Kaldfjorden Fjord. It's a popular location for campervans and recommended for viewing the northern lights (///dull.labs.venturing).

In truth, the whole area around Tromsø is a good for watching the shimmering waves of light, properly known as the aurora borealis. You can even join tours to get the best chance of spotting these aerial displays. But not when were there. The lights are a strictly September to April phenomena.

The Northern Lights (Almost)

After another light night by the fjord, we retraced our steps into Tromsø. We'd planned to look around the city centre but couldn't find anywhere to park. We did spy a parking lot in one of the underground tunnels, but its height restriction meant it was a no go for Cliff. Eventually, we parked at the Northern Lights Planetarium and science centre on the city's university campus. (///hunches.love.brighter). Parking was free because the lot isn't used by the Uni on Sundays.

We wanted to catch a planetarium show that promised to reveal all about the northern lights and waited for one of the two presentations given in English each day.

We filled time getting very hands-on in the science exhibition which occupies the same building. It's fun for kids of all ages, with interactive games, puzzles and displays on the universe, weather, the climate, energy, physics, and the human body. Highlights included calculating the impact methane-producing farm animals have on global warming – complete with sound effects. We should be far too mature to be amused by simulated flatulence, but we giggled like seven-year-olds.

Once in the planetarium, we were guided through the spectacular projection above our heads by our host – a very friendly, amusing, and informative young man. He was so enthusiastic, he sounded as though he was delivering his presentation for the very first time. We enjoyed discovering how, where, and why the aurora borealis occurs and were treated to some breathtaking film captured by obsessives who dedicate their lives to chasing the northern lights.

The unassuming car park at Tromsø planetarium turned out to be the most northerly point on our entire road trip. From there, we headed south in the general direction of the Lofoten Islands on Norway's west coast.

That Sunday afternoon, we drove for nearly three hours, skirting yet more fjords on mostly rural roads before joining the E6 – the main north-south highway that links northern Norway with western Sweden. We found yet another idyllic stopover site close to the fast-flowing Salangselva river (///lame.pots.searcher).

Norwegians take a similar approach to the Swedes when it comes to encouraging campervans and motorhomes to access the countryside. We were still careful not to break any rules, but no longer stressed about overnighting in the Scandinavian wilderness. We hunkered down on the riverbank for our tenth, budget-busting night away from official campsites.

10. THE LOFOTEN ISLANDS

After staying an extra night at our idyllic riverside camping spot, we drove through heavy rain and poor visibility for most of the day, eventually reaching a rather damp Elvelund Camping site near Sjøvegan (///huddling.referral.jeep). We tackled some long overdue laundry and gave thanks to the god of camping that there was a dryer.

It was the first campsite we'd encountered where the plug on our hook-up cable didn't fit the electric power socket on our pitch. Top Tip: make sure you have a European two-pin to camper cable adapter. We borrowed one from reception and later bought one from a camping shop for £12.

It was still overcast the next morning when we headed further south in the general direction of the Lofoten Islands.

So far in Norway, it felt as though we had been the first people to discover many of our amazing stopover locations. It was late July and we rarely had to share beauty spots with any other campers or motorhomes. However, The Lofoten Islands are a vastly different kettle of cod. (Air-dried cod, but I'll come onto that later). They're a tourist magnet.

Island Hotspot

Each summer, thousands of visitors arrive by road or ferry to explore the Lofoten Islands. Geologically speaking, the islands are the eroded tips of a three-billion-year-old, submerged mountain range. There are five main islands and hundreds of smaller ones, many linked by bridges or ferry crossings.

Together, the islands are said to resemble the foot of a lynx (the wild cat) sticking out to sea. The name "Lofoten" is derived from old Norse words for lynx and foot.

Driving through this patchwork of a landscape is a little confusing, and approaching from the north, we weren't exactly sure where the Lofotens officially began. We assumed we'd arrived when our road, route 83, ended abruptly at the Revsnes ferry terminal (/// clouds.clattered.stands).

We pulled up behind a solitary van that was parked under a gantry displaying ferry times. There was no ticket office and no sign of any staff. We guessed a tiny white spec way down the fjord was the approaching ferry, so we turned Cliff's engine off and waited.

Toll Talk

This seems a good point to talk tolls. Compared with many European countries, Norway is a toll-heavy country. Motorists are charged to use many sections of roads, particularly dual carriageways, and motorways.

To avoid having to stop and pay at toll booths every few minutes, we had signed up to the EPASS24 electronic toll payment system. We went online and entered our bank details and van registration number. This allowed roadside cameras to spot our number plate when we used toll roads and add the charge to our monthly bill.

EPASS24 is mostly used in Sweden and Norway. It's all very efficient, although you have no way of knowing how much you've spent until the payment is taken from your account towards the end of the following month. High prices meant we were having to control our spending very carefully in Norway – so having a mystery toll total was not at all helpful.

As Norwegian ferries are effectively part of the road system, the fees for using many of them can also be collected automatically by EPASS24. Our three-mile (5 km) crossing took twenty minutes and, for our 6 m (just under 20 ft) van, £5 was electronically added to our monthly total.

Once off the ferry, route 83 turned into a road again, albeit a very narrow and winding one. After a few miles, we came to a disused ferry terminal – our first stopover on what we were now confident were The Lofoten Islands (///prettiest.tomb.talkative).

Another camper was already parked beside an abandoned ticket office. A family was fishing from the jetty. It was yet another stunning location. We parked close to the edge of the old pier, overlooking the twenty-two mile (35 km) long Gullesfjorden – the fjord we'd just crossed on the ferry.

Our views up and down the vast stretch of water changed constantly. Distant mountains disappeared and reappeared as isolated patches of heavy rain passed over. The water was clear and still. Scarlet sea urchins crept slowly over submerged rocks at the water's edge. Neither of us had seen those before.

Out in the fjord, huge, swirling rings kept appearing in the water. I assumed they were caused by shoals of fish circling, just beneath the surface. No, I've no idea why they spend their evenings doing that.

There were certainly plenty of fish around. The fishing family were catching a freezer-full, gutting their catches on the quayside and throwing the nasty bits to eager seagulls.

Fishing is also included in Norway's *"allemansrätten"* (every man's right) to access the countryside. You may fish for free, without a licence, providing it's in salt water, you're on the shore or a small boat, and anything you catch is for your own consumption.

The next morning, we eventually joined the E10 – the only main road that runs north-south through the Lofoten islands. The road is like a piece of string threaded through the main islands, holding them together. It's narrow in places, twisting, turning, clinging onto mountain sides and disappearing into vast tunnels on a regular basis. The E10 may be quickest route from A to B on the Lofotens, but it's still a very scenic drive.

Henningsvær Stadium

Our next destination was a much-photographed football pitch. The stadium at Henningsvær is hallowed turf (well, synthetic grass), but it's not the home of a famous Norwegian footie club. Its fame is due to its location; on a large, levelled chunk of rock, surrounded on three sides by sea (///determining.trusteeship.purses).

To reach it, we drove through the small, island fishing village of Henningsvær. We Squeezed down the narrow main street passing tourist shops and cafes before crossing a narrow bridge to the stadium. We found a space in a small car park right beside the pitch.

While Steve launched his drone to get a bird's-eye view, I wandered around the permitter. There were no stands. Spectators take their own seats, apparently. Instead, there were rows of fish racks.

Fish – mostly cod – are hung out to dry on these wooden structures during the winter. It's an ancient and cheap way of curing without using salt. The resulting 'stockfish' are a delicacy. Once dried, they can be stored for several years. I still haven't worked out how every fish hung out to dry isn't devoured by seagulls. But the process must work because cod-curing Norwegians have used it for centuries.

We left Cliff at the stadium and enjoyed a spot of window-shopping back in the village. But there was no opportunity to stay. For the first time in Scandinavia, we'd spotted signs making it very clear that this otherwise friendly community did not tolerate overnight parking. There were "no camping" signs in abundance. The locals have clearly had their fill and no longer encourage campervans and motorhomes which, admittedly, barely fit down their narrow streets.

We searched the area around the village, but every potential overnight site had a no camping sign. We had no alternative but to check in to a formal campsite just south of Lyngvaer, beside the trusty E10 (///cassettes.fixtures.lance).

11. VIKINGS, GALES, AND A ROADSIDE RESCUE

Our second day on the Loften Islands would become a battle with the weather, though it started well enough.

Shortly after leaving our campsite, we drove over Gimsøystraumen Bridge onto the island of Gimsøy, which boasts the world's northernmost links golf course. But we weren't going for golf, we were searching for graffiti.

'Pøbel' is an anonymous, Norwegian street artist. In English, his name means hooligan. He's a Scandi version of Britain's Banksy, and his work has included spray-painting striking and slightly disturbing images on abandoned buildings on the Lofoten islands.

We eventually found the 'Butterfly House', an abandoned cottage on a deserted hillside (///friction.elect.horses). Its exterior was covered in a giant mural of a figure wearing a gas mask, looking at a butterfly delicately perched on the end of their finger. The mostly yellow artwork is a stark contrast with the natural greens and greys of the hillside. Something for the 'well, I never expected that to be there' category.

Lofoten Viking Museum

We spent the afternoon at a more mainstream attraction – the Lofoten Island's Viking Museum. It's conveniently situated right beside the E10 (///senses.cookie.magnetic). We found a space in the museum's busy car park and climbed a small hill to the entrance.

The Vikings once invaded our home city of York. We even have our own Viking Centure. So, we were intrigued to discover what spin the Norwegians would put on their home-grown marauders.

We crossed the vast open-air site towards a lake where we could see an impressive replica of a Viking longship taking tourists far out across the water. We booked two places onboard and waited patiently for the single-sailed boat to return to the jetty. Then, everything went pear-shaped.

The weather hadn't been great since we arrived on the Lofoten Islands and that afternoon, the wind suddenly became much stronger. In the middle of the lake, the Viking crew were soon struggling to keep control of their vessel. They wrestled with the huge sail, eventually lowering it, and limping back to the jetty under diesel motor power. Who knew Viking longships had those!

After the slightly ruffled passengers disembarked, the entire crew of the Viking ship operation got into an animated discussion – I assumed about whether it was safe for the next voyage go ahead. When York has its annual Viking festival, those taking part look like folks from York dressed up as fancy dress Vikings. However, this Norwegian longship crew looked like the real deal. We didn't hang around for the outcome of their debate. We abandoned the idea of a cruise and headed back up the hill to take shelter in the centrepiece of the museum – a beautifully built replica of a Viking chieftain's longhouse. It's 83 m (221 ft) long, to be exact, and a reconstruction of a building that stood on the site over a thousand years ago.

Traces of the original dwelling were discovered in 1981 when a farmer accidentally unearthed fragments of glass and pottery while ploughing a field. Further investigation revealed the remains had come from the home of a well-connected Viking chieftain, who'd made his wealth trading throughout Europe. The longhouse is a recreation of the home he shared with his family and animals.

Nearby, the museum's modern buildings bring the story of the site and its Vikings to life with artefacts and film presentations.

We spent longer at the museum than we'd intended, and it had become quite late to be finding a place to overnight. After driving to several potential sites and being confronted with yet more "no camping" signs, the only spot we could find was up a mountain.

Blown Away

In pleasant weather, the lofty perch looking down on the distant village of Unstad would have been spectacular. But with intense gusts of wind buffeting the van, it felt downright dangerous (/// thumps.stiff.laugh).

It was too late to go hunting for another location, so we found a modicum of shelter, tucking Cliff between an outcrop of rock and more of those wooden fish-drying racks. Soon, we were joined by another camper, a French motorhome and a couple who clearly thought it was the perfect spot to sleep in a car.

It became what was without doubt the worst night we've ever spent in the van. We could hear gusts of wind howling down the valley towards us before they hit us with a bang. The blinds on Cliff's windows and skylights bulged and buckled with every blast.

Around 2 am, the family in the French motorhome capitulated and set off down the narrow mountain track in the pitch darkness. Brave souls.

By morning, the gale had subsided, and we wasted no time getting off the mountain. But Cliff was not happy. A warning message lit up on his dashboard; "Start/stop not available. Check engine." The start/stop function cuts off the engine when we pause at junctions. It saves fuel and reduces emissions. The engine fires up again when you take your foot off the brake. Frankly, it gets on my wick, and I often switch it off.

But we were very worried by the "check engine" instruction because we felt we were hundreds of miles from civilisation. The last thing we wanted was a complete breakdown. So, we drove carefully to an UNO petrol station in Leknes, parked up, and called our Fiat Camper Assist helpline.

Roadside Rescue

We expected the Norwegian equivalent of a friendly AA mechanic to turn up, plug a diagnostic tool into Cliff's dash, do a bit of fiddling and send us merrily on our way. After a three hour wait, a truly enormous flat-bed truck with the word "NAF" emblazoned on its cab pulled up beside us. The driver was very friendly but told us he didn't possess a diagnostic tool. In fact, he'd never had one.

It seems Norwegian recovery services – and many others in mainland Europe – don't even attempt roadside repairs. They always prefer to scoop up your vehicle and deposit it at a garage. NAF man offered to put Cliff on the back of his lorry and leave us at the nearest Fiat Professional dealership which, despite our fears, was miraculously only a short distance away.

But it was mid-Saturday afternoon. The dealer was closed, and we didn't fancy spending the rest of the weekend in a garage parking lot.

After much discussion, hampered by the fact we speak not a syllable of Norwegian, we finally agreed that as the warning light was amber and not red, it was 'probably' ok to drive Cliff a bit further. We said we'd risk it and have Cliff checked out at the next Fiat dealership we passed on our route. This was on the understanding we would stop immediately if the warning light turned red.

World-Class Beaches

Warning light glowing, and determined not to waste the entire day, we drove very carefully to two of The Lofoten Island's most popular beaches. The first was Haukland Beach (///coconuts.latched.painters), once voted "the most beautiful beach in Europe". The judges clearly hadn't been to Robin Hoods Bay on the North Yorkshire coast, but I'll concede Haukland is dramatic. It's a crescent of white sand, flanked on one side by a mountain headland that rises directly out of the sea.

There's a short tunnel through said mountain. We drove into it and emerged near Uttakleiv Beach. This one claimed to be "The most romantic beach in Europe" (///minder.staining.react). The glow of any romanticism was somewhat tarnished by the beach charging an entry fee and being dotted with rain-soaked sheep. To be fair, we were a bit grumpy by then. It was drizzling. The sky heavy and grey. The one spec of brightness in our world was that bloomin' warning light glowing stubbornly on Cliff's dashboard. We surrendered and paid the fee for a camper parking space overlooking the rain-lashed beach.

Next morning, there was no improvement in the weather. Usually, we compare several online weather forecasts and choose to believe the most optimistic. But that morning, the apps all agreed that the rain was only going to get worse.

We *had* planned to work our way south down to Moskenes, close to the southern tip of the Lofoten Islands. From there, we'd take the four-hour ferry trip to Bodo on the mainland. This twice daily crossing is one of the most popular access points for the islands.

But the high winds that had played havoc with the Viking longship the previous day had also led to the cancellation of two full days of ferry crossings to the mainland. Delayed passengers had grabbed every available space on up-coming voyages and there were no slots available for the rest of the week.

Island Retreat

Rather than sit out the monsoon, we reluctantly decided to retrace our steps, return north, and take a less popular and shorter ferry route from Lødingen to Bognes on the mainland. There's no denying we were disappointed; not with the Lofoten Islands, just the weather. Every Norwegian we met said the conditions were very out of character for early August, but that didn't really help.

However, as we headed back up the E10, our spirits were lifted when a miracle occurred. Cliff's stop/start warning light went out. We have absolutely no idea why, and it has never come on again.

We caught the ferry at Lødingen in good time (/// printing.publisher.dent) and took a table in the café with a view over the ship's bow. We treated ourselves to a coffee but turned down the opportunity to spend £13 each on a hotdog.

The crossing took just over an hour and cost £27. We drove off the ferry at Bognes and headed south. Back on the mainland, options for free overnight parking had returned to pre-Lofoten levels and Steve found a great spot on Park4Night – a riverbank, just north of Tømmerneset, close to the site of an old sawmill (/// skyrocket.mining.district).

Today it's a tranquil spot, with no sign of the sawmill building that operated from 1800 to 1906, cutting up to three thousand logs every season. Trees arrived at the mill by river – floating twenty-three miles (37 km) from the dense forest upstream. We spotted deep grooves in the rock at the top of the nearby waterfall. We assumed they'd been gouged out by massive tree trunks sliding over the edge.

After spending a pleasant evening watching enormous fish jumping in the pool below the waterfall, we had a peaceful night – relieved to be back in the wilderness. My how things had changed.

12. THE ARCTIC CIRCLE CENTRE & TRONDHEIM TREATS

With a new day, our mood and the weather had improved. We left our secluded sawmill site and joined the E6, the main artery that runs from Norway's border with Russia to Malmo in western Sweden.

We drove for nearly three hours, through every type of landscape Norway could throw at us. Dramatic mountains softened into gentler hills and wide valleys. We hunkered into our captain's chairs and watched waterfalls, fast-flowing rivers and dense pine forests go by.

Eventually, we began a long, gentle climb through the Saltfjellet-Svartisen National Park into more open and barren tundra. Then we saw it. It looked as though a giant flying saucer had touched down not far from the roadside. This was Norway's Arctic Circle Centre.

The Arctic Circle Centre

Technically, we'd been inside the Arctic Circle for the last couple of weeks. The Swedes had made no song and dance about it when we entered it a couple of weeks earlier. But here, at 66' 33" North, was a full-blown visitor experience. The circle's imaginary line passes through the middle of the UFO-shaped building (/// reserve.adapt.tidy). It's a point where the sun never sets on June 21st and never rises on the 21st of December.

We left Cliff in the car park beside a campervan converted from a ginormous, ex-army truck. It had tyres taller than us and a ladder up to its lofty accommodation box. Crouching in the shadow of this behemoth, Cliff looked somewhat emasculated.

The Arctic Circle Centre turned out to be a mix of educational experience and coach-trip tourist attraction. Displays and films explained the ecosystem of the polar region and its landscape. The gift shop offered Norwegian jumpers, elk keyrings, "I love Norway" stickers and toy reindeer. Kids loved a family of animated trolls and were terrified by a stuffed polar bear, said to be the largest ever found in Europe. For the record, there are no live polar bears in mainland Norway.

Steve treated me to lunch in the centre's Reindeer Bistro. I opted for reindeer sausages and mash. He chose reindeer stew. It was certainly an experience: "I ate reindeer sausages in the arctic circle" etc. But if they ever appear on the shelves at Tesco, I'll probably give them a miss.

After our visit, we continued a further fifty miles (80km) south and found another hilltop stopover overlooking the city of Mo i Rana (/// yarn.sorters.readjust).

That night, I was surprised to discover, online, that the arctic circle is on the move. It edges north about 4.5 m (48 ft) every year. This is down to something beyond my comprehension involving fluctuations in the angle of the Earth's axis. So, top tip: visit the Arctic Circle Centre… while it is still in the Arctic Circle.

Apart from mentioning the £13 hotdogs on the Lødingen to Bognes ferry, I've said little about Norway being expensive. It is. Very. We hardly ever ate out in Norway in fear of blowing our £60 daily allowance. But our grocery cupboards were bare, and we needed a big shop.

Border Hopping Shopping

Rather than take out a mortgage to buy provisions locally, we left the country. We hopped over the border into Sweden and took the E12 to Umfors where there's a Gränslöst supermarket (///perks.keeper.happen). Such border dashes are quite common among Norwegians. They even arrange coach trips to cash in on Sweden's lower prices.

The supermarket's high shelves and narrow aisles were packed with all the supplies we could wish for. We spent £110, filled Cliff's shelves, and dashed back over the border. I say 'border' – it was just a sign saying Norge at the side of the road.

After re-joining the E6, we found an official, free campervan stop just south of Majavatn (///tearfully.suspect.mulls).

The Gateway To The North

The following day involved a relentless drive south for 175 miles. We made a brief stop at "The Gateway to North" (///blazing.furniture.bulges) where an archway over the road symbolises the divide between the north and south of Norway.

The arch depicts the northern lights and provides a backdrop for many a selfie. Otherwise, it's just a useful place to take a break. There's a café, shop, and toilets - Norway's equivalent of Watford Gap.

By the end of the day, we had covered almost four thousand miles on our adventure and parked for the night in a car park overlooking Trondheim Fjord (///crab.earphones.meaning).

Trondheim

After several days in the wilderness, we were ready for another taste of civilisation. Trondheim is a smart, university city and a world player in developing environmentally friendly technologies. Its historic centre attracts lots of tourists – and that amounts to a red flag in our book. So, we did our usual trick of trying to find free parking on the outskirts and taking public transport into the centre. Our campervanning apps produced few choices, so we settled for a car park which had no bus or train stops nearby (///figs.donor.layers) and walked.

Fjord-side paths led us inland towards Trondheim harbour, and we were soon in a distinctly industrial part of the docks. A giant, concrete structure on the waterside looked like the lair of a Bond villain, complete with pens built to shelter submarines. Tourist information signs revealed they were indeed pens for sheltering U-boats (///buzz.sublet.scam).

Germany built the complex, using slave labour, during its occupation of Norway in the Second World War. It was HQ for the thirteenth U-boat flotilla and part of the largest German naval base in Northern Europe. "DORA" Bunker One held 16 U-boats. A second bunker was unfinished when the war ended.

This slightly sinister building is unmissable, but we saw nothing to suggest it was being promoted as an attraction. Low-key signage simply explained what it had been. Most of the building is now the Trondheim city archive. Its 3m (10 ft) thick walls protect important documents - not deadly submarines.

You can camp overnight in the shadow of the giant bunker if that takes your fancy. There's designated camper parking, with facilities, just across the road (///press.avid.asserts). The camper park was almost full when we walked past, but if you could bag a space, it would give you easy access to Trondheim centre.

Our walking route soon became much smarter. There were trendy cafes and bars in old dockside buildings, and more people whizzing around on electric scooters than we'd seen anywhere before. We crossed the river via a footbridge and slipped into tourist mode in the historic city centre.

We took snaps of the multi-coloured wharf buildings that flank the river. The originals were built in the 1500s to store sugar and grain but were destroyed in the great fire of Trondheim in 1681. Today's blue, red, orange, and green replacements contain smart shops, bistros, and riverside apartments.

Uphill Struggle

We crossed Trondheim's quirky Old Town Bridge to the foot of a steep hill. We were about to start our climb to the seventeenth century Kristiansten Fortress but were side-tracked by some unexpected entertainment (///anyway.forest.inclined).

The hill features an intriguing invention - a moving belt sunk into the ground that propels cyclists to the summit at a rate of knots. Or rather, it would, if anyone could master using it.

In theory, you sit on your bike, keeping your left foot on the pedal. Then, you place your right foot on a starting position which is marked on the ground. Next, you hit the "go" button. This makes a footplate appear that's attached to the moving belt. Your foot *should* end up on the footplate and remain there as the plate hurtles to the top of the hill taking you and your bike with it. The reality? Most people fall off the second the plate heads off up the hill.

Kristiansten Fortress

We were overtaken by several empty cycle lift footplates as we walked up the incline. At the summit, we explored the fortress – a defensive stronghold that saved Trondheim from a Swedish invasion in 1718 and was occupied Nazi forces during World War II. A chapel stands close to where 23 Norwegian wartime resistance fighters were executed.

Even if you're not into military history, it's worth visiting the fort for its spectacular views of the surrounding mountains, fjords, the city, and its cathedral.

Trondheim Cathedral

Nidaros Cathedral was built over the tomb of St Olav – the Viking king who converted Norway to Christianity. It fell into disrepair in the Middle Ages and what you see today is mostly the result of an ongoing restoration programme that began in 1869.

We were most interested in the cathedral's west front, one of the most recent parts to be renovated (///stepping.pelting.remind). It's covered in over sixty statues of saints, prophets, and Norwegian kings – plus a whole menagerie in stone including elephants, donkeys, bears, and bees. The whole spectacle comes under the watchful eyes of Archangel Gabriel whose face was made to look like Bob Dylan. The sculptor bestowed the honour to acknowledge Dylan's opposition to the Vietnam War.

13. DRIVES OF OUR LIVES

The following day, the terrain changed as we made our way southwest towards Norway's Atlantic coast. Narrow valleys between almost vertical cliffs gave way to a flatter, gentler landscape. After driving for a couple of hours, we found a spot to camp near the Gjemnessund suspension bridge (///downward.lectures.handbag).

Access was from a service station at the northern end of the bridge. A narrow, overgrown track with many potholes and a sharp hairpin bend took us down to the water's edge. We parked close to what looked like an abandoned fishing pier with a magnificent view (///admires.level.diplomas).

All Calm In Kristiansund

The following day, we re-joined the main road to the seaport of Kristiansund (not to be confused with Kristiansand – with an "a" - on the south coast of Norway). We found free parking beside a skateboard park (///organist.mason.rebel) and strolled into town.

Kristiansund is spread over four small islands. It is famous for its colourful houses, an opera house, and the production of klipfish -

salted cod, which is split and dried on rocks.

We'd already noticed that rural Norway was sparsely populated. Over half of its 5.5 million citizens live in the south in the region around the capital, Oslo. But we were genuinely surprised that on a Saturday lunchtime, even a medium-sized town like Kristiansund looked deserted. It felt shut down – like Sundays used to be in Britain before the law allowed our shops to open on the Sabbath.

We watched a handful of people climb on board the 'sound boat', a ferry which does a twenty-minute round trip of the islands (/// porch.eggplants.reserves). This ferry has a claim to fame. It's the world's oldest, motorised, regular transport system that has been in continuous service - no less. But Kristiansund's main streets were almost empty. The only shop doing any kind of trade was an establishment that's unique to Norway – a Vinmonopolet, or wine monopoly.

A Sobering Experience

Norway's attitude to alcohol can be rather sobering for visitors from the UK. Simply, the Norwegians charge a lot for booze and have strict controls on where and when it's sold.

You may buy most alcoholic drinks in bars, but supermarkets or service stations are not allowed to sell anything with an alcohol content of over 4.7%. These outlets may sell weaker beers and lagers but certainly no wine or spirits.

Stronger alcohol is only sold in the Vinmonopolets which are owned, licensed, and run by the state. There's usually only one outlet per town. They're open 9am to 8pm Monday to Friday, close at 6pm on Saturdays and don't open at all on Sundays.

They never advertise or offer discounts or have promotions. This alone would put a stopper up our customary approach to selecting a bottle of wine. Intrigued, we popped into Kristiansund's wine monopoly, and I had a quick chat with the manager.

"In the UK, you treat buying alcohol like buying milk," he told me. "You can get it at the petrol station - anywhere. Norway just doesn't do it like that."

Make someone feel like a complete alcoholic why don't you!

The restrictions date back over a century to a period when Norway had a range of social problems that led many of its citizens to hit the bottle. And while the tight controls on alcohol feel very restrictive to us Brits, a survey carried out in 2016 revealed eighty percent of Norwegians are perfectly happy with the situation.

After returning to Cliff at the skate park, we took a short journey to an official campsite - Atlanterhavsveien Sjøstuer (/// blackmail.thrasing.never). We needed to use its laundry, but the main reason for picking this site was its proximity to a section of coastal road that had been on our travel bucket list for years – The Atlantic Highway.

The Atlantic Highway

Blame James Bond. This dramatic stretch of coastal road was the setting for a breathtaking car chase in the 007 blockbuster *A Time to Die*. It took six years to build the road and construction was interrupted by no less than twelve hurricanes. It's that kind of terrain.

Now, this dramatic strip of asphalt zigzags between eight wave-battered islands, dipping, arching, and flipping over as many bridges.

Next morning, we were up early and approached the Highway from the north. Mr Bond tackled it in a Toyota Landcruiser, pursued by villains in high-speed Range Rovers and Land Rover Discoveries. It was no less thrilling to tackle it in something resembling a parcel delivery van.

The official section of highway covers only five miles (8.3 km) - much shorter than it looks in the movie sequences and car ads filmed along it. Steve had the first drive which felt over before it began. So, we took turns behind the wheel, covering the full length of the highway several times.

The greatest thrill was climbing and topping the Storseisundet Bridge, the highest bridge on the route. Locals call it 'the drunk bridge' (/// hands.lilac.huddle). It's both an engineering triumph and an optical illusion. It climbs steeply to a height of around 75 ft (23 m) above the water, then bends sharply at the summit, giving you the sensation you're about to drive off a diving board.

The Atlantic Highway cost nearly £9 million to build and tolls were introduced to help pay for it. But after ten years, the investment had been recovered and this spectacular stretch of road is now toll free.

It was a terrific way to spend part of a sunny Sunday morning in August. But it can be a very different story in winter. The exposed highway has zero protection from fierce winds and giant breakers that smash in from the Atlantic. I'm glad we got to ride the rollercoaster during the relative calm of summer. But we had another daredevil drive to come.

On The Trail Of The Trolls

After heading inland for a couple of hours, we came to another road on our bucket list – the Trollstigen pass. This serpentine road clings to the side of a mountain, has eleven hairpin bends, gradients of ten per cent and waterfalls crashing down the rock face.

We knew we were getting close when signs warned us of trolls on the road. "Trollstigen" means the troll's path or trail. Trolls are a big part of Norwegian folklore - ugly, mythical creatures that live in the forests and prefer to stomp about at night because sunlight turns them into stone. They can have up to three heads and sometimes just one eye. Charming creatures.

Before we made our ascent, we pulled into Gjestegården (////// slugs.stuffy.vibe), effectively a troll centre, close to the foot of the pass. It has a souvenir shop, a restaurant and a campsite that welcomes campervans and motorhomes. We bought a pair of disgusting toy trolls to give our godson and his sister the heebie-jeebies when we got home, then climbed into Cliff to tackle our first climb. Steve was behind the wheel for our first ascent.

We would find ourselves on many serpentine roads throughout Europe during our year-long adventure, but Trollstigen was our first and I reckon the best.

The pass is at the end of a valley. As you approach, it looks as though the road is about to run out. But look upwards and you'll see it continues in a death-defying zigzag up the side of the mountain.

The ascent began gently enough, but soon we were climbing steeply. In places, the road is hardly more than single track with occasional passing places. There was space for cars to squeeze past our van, but not much. Passing involved us teetering on the edge of a sheer drop or being squeezed against a rock face.

We were doing well in the bravery department until a coach full of tourists hurtled down the pass towards us. Some buses have trouble on the hairpins. Not this one. The driver threw it round the corner with the confidence of a man who had clearly never watched the end of *The Italian Job*.

The Trollstigen pass took eight years to build and was opened in 1939. It's been upgraded countless times since. Barriers have been introduced to prevent rock falls, but the route is essentially as steep and twisting as it ever was.

About halfway up, the spectacular Stigfossen waterfall crashes down close to the road. The views back along the valley become more magnificent the higher you climb. Eventually, the road stops twisting and plateaus at 2,300 ft (700 m), just before you come to the Trollstigen visitor centre (///clapper.reckon.crypt).

Beaming from ear to ear, Steve was keen to see if Trollstigen was as exciting going down, so we made our descent before I got a chance to drive a remarkably well-behaved Cliff back up to the top again.

A short walk from the visitor centre there's a viewing platform protruding from the rock face (///stays.fizzy.wriggled). The bird's eye view of the pass is not to be missed.

After a day that would have delighted the grumpiest of TV motor show presenters, we parked up for the night in the visitor centre car park which, surprisingly, was free of charge. Just one word of caution; if you're planning to visit Trollstigen, it is usually closed from October to mid-May. The precise dates vary depending on the weather conditions each year, so check online before you commit to driving to this thrilling but sometimes inhospitable part of Norway.

14. MOUNTAIN CLIMBING IN A CAMPERVAN

We woke in the car park at the Trollstigen visitor centre to the sound of English voices. Something we'd not heard for nearly six weeks. Two young men had spent the night a few metres away from us in a tiny roof tent on top of an old Fiat Panda. The two pals had bought their car for about £200 and were heading home after driving thousands of miles through countless countries for charity. One had taken time off studying; the other had given up his job to go on the adventure.

We'd discovered later, via Instagram, that their cut-price camping setup didn't survive much longer. The wheel fell off their Fiat a few weeks later and the inspiring young travellers had to make alternative arrangements to get home.

The Adblue Blues

Talking of Fiats, after climbing Trollstigen (twice) Cliff's AdBlue warning light came on. AdBlue is the magic liquid that some modern diesels squirt into their exhaust emissions to make them less polluting. The warning light meant we were running low on the additive and needed to top up.

As we left Trollstigen and headed to the town of Linge, we found a fuel station and replenished the AdBlue tank. However, the warning light stayed on. It should go out after a refill.

Clearly, this led to an enormous amount of stress. If you run out of AdBlue completely, your engine won't start again. We knew the AdBlue tank was almost full, but Cliff was still insisting it was about to run dry and started counting down the miles to when the engine would not restart. Where in this desolate part of Norway would we get this fixed? We drove on for a couple of hours, genuinely worried that we were going to end up stranded.

Then lo! After many miles, another miracle. The light just went out. We clutched at straws for an explanation. Was it the altitude? Had Trollstigen put too much strain on the engine? We had no idea. Cliff never did that to us again, but our trust in FIAT electronics had taken another nosedive.

After catching a ferry from Linge (///robes.intruding.pursuing) to Eidsal, we continued on country road 63 towards Geiranger and found ourselves at the top of another steep, 11-hairpin descent - the so-called Eagle Road. We paused at the Ørnesvingen viewpoint to soak up the magnificent panorama over the town of Geiranger tucked away at the eastern head of the fjord (///excavate.marbles.balancing).

Geiranger

Geiranger is a popular destination for cruise ships touring the Norwegian fjords. We could see one of these giant vessels docked at its cruise terminal. The ship dominated the village. It was difficult to imagine how it had navigated the fjord, let alone manoeuvred into what, from our vantage point, looked like a model village.

We enjoyed the descent down the Eagle Road. It's not as dramatic as Trollstigen, but still puts a vehicle through its paces. Car companies use it for winter testing and improving ride and handling. At the bottom, we stopped by the fjord for a spot of lunch.

As we munched our cheese and tuna toasties, groups of tourists whizzed past, skimming over the water surface in high-speed dinghies. These fifty-minute fjord tours depart from Geiranger and cost £50 per person. I guess they're popular with cruise ship escapees, but we preserved our daily budget and gave it a miss.

After lunch, we drove through the narrow streets of Geiranger. It was certainly one of the smartest and busiest towns we'd seen in Norway so far. Around 250 people live there permanently, but the town attracts several hundred thousand visitors during the summer months.

Steep-sided mountains tower above the village on three sides. We discovered later that large cracks have appeared in some of those mountains and there's the constant risk that huge sections of rock could crash into the fjord creating a tsunami. Early warning sirens have been installed in Geiranger to give people enough time to evacuate. We didn't stop in the town; we were about to go mountaineering.

Our Mountain Climbing Camper.

Climbing Trollstigen the previous afternoon had felt like a drive into the sky. But our next destination was twice as high – the top of Dalsnibba mountain, about 1500 m (almost five-thousand feet) above sea level.

As a very adventurous crow would fly, the summit is just over four miles (7 km) from Geiranger village. But climbing to that height in a campervan involves another journey on serpentine roads that's three times as far. Scaling a mountain in the comfort of a campervan swivel chair is only possible because of the remarkable Nibbevegen road.

It's a private toll road that was completed in 1939, but not opened until 1948 because of the Second World War. We paid £23 at a toll booth and began our climb to the summit. Many hairpins later we reached the top – a dead end at the Geiranger skywalk.

We parked at the visitor centre (///tribes.brains.crunches) and joined the crowds on a viewing platform that protrudes from the mountain top. Astounding doesn't do justice to the view we had on that clear afternoon. It's a 360-degree panorama, with snow-capped mountain peaks in every direction. It's a true, high-mountain experience even though you've not had to take a single step to get there. I try not to overuse the word, but it was awesome.

The mountain-top visitor centre had a restaurant and shop. There was also a car park just below the summit where several campers and motorhomes had already parked up for the night (/// levels.trembles.suffice). We joined them and had the best view we'd ever seen through a campervan windscreen (See chapter main photo). Such views aren't guaranteed. The weather can change quickly at this altitude. And that's exactly what it did.

Heavy wind and rain woke us several times that night. The following morning, I took down the blind from the windscreen to reveal... no view whatsoever. We were shrouded in mist – or was it cloud? There was no way we were going to risk driving down those hairpins in zero visibility.

I ventured out to take some video of the extreme weather conditions, expecting to be stuck on the mountain until the mist cleared. But suddenly, headlights appeared. A coach filled with tourists emerged out of the greyness, followed by a German motorhome which parked right beside Cliff. The couple who climbed out said the route up Dalsnibba had been clear, apart from the last few hundred metres. We were in narrow band of thick cloud.

Fog lights on, we set off down the mountain. Sure enough, after a couple of minutes, the cloud disappeared, and we had a clear run all the way down the mountain. I should mention that winter weather conditions mean the toll road up Dalsnibba is usually closed from October to the end of May.

Once down from the mountain, we drove on to Gotli (/// sediment.reinforce.lifetimes) and turned onto one of Norway's official scenic routes, the 258 Gamle Strunefjellsvegan to Videseater road.

This ancient road twists through a harsh, treeless landscape. For many sections, it's single track, often lined with hand-cut marker stones and riddled with potholes.

The route is relatively flat, and we didn't realise how high we still were until the road dropped into a deep valley. We flanked a fast-flowing river that cascaded down the mountain in a ladder of impressive waterfalls.

At the bottom, the landscape softened, and the air was noticeably warmer. We drove through several smart towns and villages that would not have looked out of place on the French Riviera. The area had a much softer feel than the previous places we'd visited in Norway.

In Stryn, we found an unexpected bonus – a campervan and motorhome service point where we filled up with fresh water and disposed of our grey and black waste for free (///freshest.cried.cardinal). These useful facilities pop up throughout Scandinavia. The popular camper travel apps will help you find them.

Beyond Stryn, we started looking for a place to park for the night. Our plan was to find a free site close to the Briksdalsbreen Glacier that we intended to visit the next morning. Others must have had the same idea as several overnight spots recommended on our apps were already full. We eventually settled for a roadside car park bordering Lake Oldevatnet (///flux.smarting.sharper). We were a little unsure if camping was allowed, but three more vans arrived shortly after us, so we decided to chance it. Safety in numbers!

15. THE MEGA-TUNNEL AND THE SNOW ROAD

From our car park camping spot, we thought we could just see the Briksdalsbreen Glacier – a tiny, mouthwash-blue wedge between two mountain tops on the distant horizon. But we weren't sure. We'd never seen a glacier before.

We set off towards it, our road first hugging the lakeside, then a fast-flowing river; meltwater from the glacier, we assumed. We were clearly in camping country. There were more campsites than we'd seen anywhere on our travels through Scandinavia. Eventually, we arrived at the Briksdalsbreen visitor centre (///innocence.inherit.headed).

The centre is glacier base camp. It has a restaurant, shop and parking for cars and coaches. You can hike up a mountain road to the star attraction, but we decided to travel by 'troll car'. These vehicles look like converted golf buggies and whizz you 2.5 km (a mile and a half) up the mountain track to a drop-off point that's a ten-minute walk from the glacier's edge (///infants.unafraid.install).

We bought our tickets (about £23 each), and along with six other tourists, climbed onboard the first troll car that became available. Our driver threw the open-topped buggy into gear and bolted off up the hill. It was raining, so we were already slightly damp. Driving through the spray from a waterfall completed our saturation.

The path from the drop-off point took us through woodland. It was a little uneven, but far less treacherous than some online reviews had suggested. We emerged from the trees to be confronted by a large, milky green pool and, beyond, a rock face. In a giant, V-shaped groove at the top of the rocks was the glacial ice. It looked as though a torrent of icy blue water had been frozen by a magic spell, seconds before it was about to plunge over the edge.

The scene would have been more spectacular in better weather, but it was nonetheless fascinating. Like many other visitors, I just stood in the drizzle and stared. Information notices nearby helped explain what we were gawping at.

Glaciers are ancient chunks of ice. Most were formed in the last ice age from layers of compacted snow. They survive, providing the ice that melts in summer is less than the ice that forms in winter. Sincere apologies to glaciologists for that rather simplistic explanation.

Most glaciers are in regions that are unreachable – at least for tourists. Although we couldn't walk on the *Briksdalsbreen* glacier, or get close enough to touch it, it is one of most accessible glaciers on the planet. But perhaps not for long.

Studies have predicted that global warning could result in half of the world's glaciers melting by the end of the century. Markers along the woodland pathway back to the troll cars showed where the edge of the glacier had reached in previous decades – unmistakable evidence that it is shrinking.

Aboard An Eco-Ferry

Later that afternoon, we came across an example of how Norway is serious about saving the planet. We were travelling along national road five when we plunged into the Amla Tunnel. Nothing unusual about that in Norway. But when we emerged from the mountain, the road ended abruptly at the Mannheller ferry terminal (/// proudest.mats.trunk).

We were taking ferry crossings in our stride by now and spotted nothing unusual about the rather smart ferry we drove onto - until it started moving. It was silent: one of a growing number of Norwegian ferries that run mostly or entirely on electricity. Our hybrid ferry shuttled up to 120 cars and around four hundred passengers across Sognefjord – Norway's longest and deepest fjord - mostly on battery power.

The boat re-charges during the brief time it's docked, plugging into the Norwegian ferry equivalent of giant rapid phone charger. Norway is aiming for all its ferries to be electric by 2030.

The Borgund Stave Church

Our high-tech, planet-saving crossing took around fifteen minutes. After disembarking at Fodnes, we soon joined the E16 route to visit something altogether more ancient.

Old churches don't usually top my 'must visit' list, but the Borgund Stave Church is something else (/// leads.fatigued.simulator). It's all black, made of wood and looks more like the home of a wicked witch than a place of worship. It has a seven-tiered roof. Imagine several black sheds have dropped out of the sky and piled up on top of each other, and you'll get the picture. The upper roofs are decorated with carved, wooden dragons, apparently to ward off evil spirits.

It's thought the Borgund church was built between 1180 and 1250 and one of over 1300 such churches in Norway. It's well worth a visit, simply because it's so weird.

That night, we camped a short distance from the stave church on the old King's Road, a historical hiking trail that was once a main route between the east and west of Norway. (///

paddock.freezing.thrashing).

A Record-Breaking Tunnel

Visting the stave church had taken us a little out on a limb, so next morning, we did some backtracking before we could enjoy yet more driving extremes. Our first destination was a mind-boggling tunnel.

There are over 1200 road tunnels in Norway, but the one between Lærdal and Aurland is the undisputed daddy. At just over fifteen miles (24 km) long, the Lærdal is the longest road tunnel in the world. Only the Gotthard Base Tunnel in Switzerland is longer, but that's just for trains. We entered Lærdal at its northern end (///dive.greyhound.lively).

It's the scale of the tunnel that's so impressive, not just its physical dimensions, but the vision, engineering and investment that went into creating it. This epic hole in the ground was built to improve the main road between Norway's biggest cities, Bergen, and Oslo. The planners wanted the route to be free of ferry crossings to minimise delays. So, Norway spent the equivalent of around £68 million drilling 2.5 million cubic metres or rock out of a mountain range and building a road through it.

The Lærdal has no escape tunnels. High-tech monitoring ensures it is one of the safest tunnels in the world. It has no ventilation shafts either: a sophisticated filtration system removes pollutants from the air as it flows from one end of the tunnel to the other. To avoid monotony, and the danger of driver's nodding off at the wheel, there are gentle curves. Every four miles (6 km), the underground roadway opens into vast chambers, lit with coloured lights. There are regular parking bays plus areas large enough for coaches to turn round, without reversing, in case of emergencies. After being overwhelmed by Norway's natural beauty for days, it was a refreshing change to marvel at a man-made wonder.

Having driven under a mountain range for about twenty minutes, our next challenge was to go back over the top of it – on the old mountain pass the tunnel had replaced.

The Stegastein Viewpoint

After leaving the tunnel, we drove through the small holiday village of Aurlandsvangen and began our ascent up one of the trickiest roads we'd encounter on our travels.

The route is known as Aurlandsfjellet, or 'The Snow Road' - another of Norway's eighteen designated scenic routes. We were hairpin experts by now. The once horrifying combination of sharp bends and sheer drops down mountain sides no longer spooked us. The challenge with *this* road was that it was narrow and busy.

Most of the route is just wide enough for a single car. There *are* passing places, but not many. If you're in a camper and meet an oncoming vehicle, one of you must inevitably back up. When the second vehicle is another campervan or motorhome, it's even trickier. When small convoys of vehicles meet head on, it's a nightmare.

We were stuck in one multi-vehicle log jam for at least ten minutes. Every driver caught up in it tried shuffling their vehicle to release the blockage. There's almost no room to manoeuvre when you have a rock face or trees almost scraping your van on one side and a death-defying drop off the mountain on the other. I have no idea what eventually allowed our traffic clot to break up, but it did.

The road gets busy in summer because it leads to The Stegastein Viewpoint, which attracts tourists like flies (///genius.pickle.cardinal). When we reached the lookout, the car parks were overflowing so we parked on a verge.

The viewpoint is a wood and steel walkway that protrudes 31 m (100 ft) from the side of the mountain. We waited for our turn to stand at the end, where a glass barrier improves your view while giving you the distinct impression you're about to fall to your death.

Once you've overcome the queasiness, the view across to snow-capped mountains and to the Aurlands fjord over 650 m (two-thousand feet) below takes your breath away.

From the viewpoint, we could have continued along the snow road to Lærdal, completing a circle back to where we'd entered the mega tunnel. But as we'd been there and done that, we gritted our teeth and headed back down the serpentine road which felt even steeper on the descent than it had on the way up.

The Norwegians attempt to keep the route from Aurlandsfjorden to the Stegastein Viewpoint open all year round, but the rest of the snow road is closed in winter.

With two more great driving experiences under our belts, we rejoined the E16 highway and headed for 'The Capital of the Fjords', Bergen. We got as far as Åsane on the outskirts and couldn't resist the temptation to spend another free overnight, courtesy of the flat-pack furniture maestros, IKEA (///insisting.overt.speared).

16. DINOSAURS AND DEEP-SEA DISASTERS

After a peaceful night in the IKEA car park, we treated ourselves to breakfast in the store. As we watched the rain streaking down the restaurant windows, we spontaneously dropped our plan to visit Bergen – even though we could have taken a free IKEA shuttle bus from the store into city centre. It was just too wet and miserable.

It ended up being a big driving day and, for only the second time in seven weeks on the road, felt a bit bored and more than a little frustrated.

Norway is a long, narrow country. From north to south, it's just over a thousand miles (1,752 km). If you hung a duplicate Norway from the bottom of the existing one, it would reach the Mediterranean. We'd travelled well into the Arctic Circle, so I guess we should have expected a long drive back.

Norway's main highways are superb. They're wide, open, and incredibly well-maintained. We paid tolls to travel on many of them, and given their quality, I had no beef about that. What I found so frustrating on the larger roads were the speed limits.

Nowhere In Norway Fast

We spent most of our time on Norway's country roads where the speed limit is usually 49.7 mph (80 km/h). On dual carriageways and most motorways, it's usually 56 mph (90 km/h). On the motorway stretches where the limit goes up to 100 km/h, we felt like we were flying. But even that's only 62 miles per hour.

I'm not a speed freak, honest. But with vast distances to travel on mostly deserted motorways, the Norwegian limits left me with steam coming out of my ears.

I appreciate it's about safety in a country that's covered in ice and snow for much of the year. Norway also has more than its fair share of mists, high winds, winter darkness, long tunnels, and enormous lumps of rock beside the carriageway that would always win if you picked a fight with them.

The Norwegian's cautious approach to speed works. Statistically, Norway is one of the safest places to drive in the world. All I'm saying is, if you do take a long tour through the country, allow for motorway journeys to take much longer than you might expect.

Once we left the main roads, our spirits were uplifted when we discovered a free service point for disposing of toilet waste. We're easily pleased. The facility was in the in the village of Fitjar on county road 545 – unusually, at the town's fire station.

The welcome re-fresh allowed us to stay off-grid, so we parked up in the tiny fishing port of Mosterhamn, on an abandoned jetty close to the mouth of the picturesque harbour (///glider.rainwater.unfilled).

Next morning, we made good progress down the E39 coastal road, took yet another ferry from Arsvågen to Mortavika and found free on-street parking in a suburb of Stavanger (///affords.after.tallest). We walked to the city's harbour and found what we were searching for – the Norwegian Petroleum Museum. (///bunny.endings.milder).

An Oily Story

Trust me, this is another of those attractions that is far more interesting than it sounds. It's the story of oil; how it's formed; how it's extracted from the North Sea and how it's responsible for Norway's financial security.

The modern, museum looks like a mini oil-rig complex on the waterfront. We were welcomed inside by hordes of full-size, animatronic dinosaurs. These roaring, snarling monsters had absolutely nothing to do with oil. But they were around in the Jurassic period when the organic materials that became oil were laid down – the prefect excuse to pack a museum with robotic dinosaurs. Kids loved them.

More on-subject exhibits included giant models of deep-sea oil platforms, diving bells and rescue vessels, plus colossal pieces of underwater drilling kit. The museum is very transparent about the dangers of North Sea oil exploration, telling the story of major disasters and the investigations and safety improvements that followed them. There's also a hi-tech immersive experience which takes you on a journey to the bottom of the sea – and below.

You won't discover much about economics in this book, but one financial story told at the Petroleum Museum deserves a mention. After discovering its oilfields in the late 1960s, Norway didn't squander its oil profits. Instead, the state-owned Statoil company stashed the cash in a giant investment fund which has grown into an enormous piggybank-cum/financial safety blanket for the whole nation. It's the oldest sovereign wealth fund in the world and now valued at around 1.4 trillion dollars.

This mega rainy-day fund is managed cautiously but is probably a key factor in Norway being able to afford free university places, forty-nine weeks of paid parental leave and a generous welfare state system. It will also provide an income long after the country's oil runs out or is replaced by greener energies.

Multi-Coloured Old Town

A short walk from the museum took us to the more traditional attractions of Stavanger's old town. Its wooden houses, cafes and smart shops are painted in bright colours – quite a shock to the eyeballs after being immersed in the blues and greens of Norway's fjords and mountains for weeks.

Our stroll through the town was cut short when, for some unaccountable reason, I did my back in. This is not something that usually happens to me, and I've no idea what suddenly gave me intense pain and difficulty standing upright, let alone walking. I mention this unfortunate episode, not for sympathy, but to share that buying 500 mg of paracetamol and a tube of pain-relieving gel from a Stavanger chemist cost £32. No sign of a subsidy from the oil profits slush fund on that occasion.

It took me nearly an hour to hobble back to the van. After a short drive through the city, we came to Mollebutka Parking – a recently-built overnight parking spot on the outskirts of Stavanger which was already busy with campervans and motorhomes (/// nozzles.expert.routines).

Three Swords In A Rock

The site was beside Hafrsfjord, a modest fjord by Norwegian standards, and a popular recreation area. A short stroll along the shoreline took us to its most striking feature – three giant bronze swords with their tips buried in a rock.

The 10 m (33 ft) sculpture commemorates a key point in Norway's history – the unification of the country under King Harald Fairhair after he thwarted several other regional kings in a naval battle in 872. The tallest sword represents Harald, the two smaller ones, the defeated kings.

Next morning, we headed for Stavanger airport, not for a medevac flight home to sort my back out, but to visit what we'd heard was a stunning beach at the end of the runway. (My back was much better thanks).

We stopped in a large, free car park close to the beach (///intention.submit.claim). One large sign made it clear that overnight stays were *not* allowed. Another shouted "No Kitesurfing" – presumably to prevent kite-surfers becoming entangled with aircraft.

The beach was almost deserted, apart from a few standard surfers not attached to kites. It was windy and fresh. Cobwebs well and truly blown away, we returned to the van for another long drive.

Our destination was Kristiansand – for no other reason than my Mum had been there and was bound to ask us what we thought of it. We headed south, following the 'sea' route which turned out to have hardly any views of the sea at all. So, we re-joined the E39. I've moaned enough about speed limits already, but this was another journey that dragged.

Just before Kristiansand, we used our trusty apps to find a free overnight stop at a picnic site. Perched on a ledge beside a small road bridge, our view over yet another fjord and its patchwork of tiny islands was what we'd come to expect from Norway. It was stunning. (///maker.counters.conspired).

17. FLOATING SAUNAS AND £12 PINTS

The next day dawned bright and sunny, and we set off in good time for the seaside city of Kristiansand on the southern tip of Norway. It's a popular stop-off for Norwegian cruises.

We parked at "Stampa Parkering" beside a large nature park and recreation area just north of the city (///biggest.blaring.alone). After securing the van, we took an enjoyable stroll through the parkland, weaving around its many lakes and pools. We gradually dropped down the wooded hillside and emerged close to Kristiansand's tourist centre.

We had no plans. We were in mooch mode. So, when we saw a free organ recital was about to start in Kristiansand's cathedral, we tagged onto a line of people filing inside. Risking something different paid off. The half-hour concert was brilliant, thanks to an exceptionally talented organist and the mighty sound of his instrument filling what, by cathedral standards, was a relatively small and intimate space.

Kristiansand felt busier, more open, and more sophisticated than the towns we'd visited in the north. Shops around the Cathedral were distinctly 'designer'. There were plenty of tax-free offers, presumably targeted at people on day release from cruise ships.

We found our way to the old fish market (///bench.isolated.paper) and treated ourselves to lunch at one of the many waterside restaurants. Fishcakes - a welcome change from ham and cheese toasties in the van.

Our return to Cliff took us back up the hill and through the park. By then, the sun had tempted several people into its large bathing lake. We nipped back to the van, grabbed our swim shorts, and took a surprisingly pleasant dip in the lake ourselves. As we bobbed about in the lukewarm water, we had a strategy meeting and agreed to head east in the general direction of Norway's capital, Oslo.

When we left Kristiansand, Cliff's trip counter showed we'd driven nearly 2,300 miles (3,700 km) in Norway - almost half the total distance we'd travelled since we'd left home less than eight weeks before. We reckoned we'd stayed at official campsites for only two nights in Norway. That was made possible by the country's 'right to roam' policy and the generous provision of camper service points.

Generally, camper app guru Steve had no difficulties finding stopovers. But as we we'd approached Norway's south coast it had become more of challenge. Fewer off-grid suggestions came up on his phone. We assumed the change was because we'd reached Norway's most densely populated region.

That evening, we searched harder than usual to find an overnight location. Eventually we settled in a forest clearing beside country road 363, northeast of Helle (///brambles.thinnest.grounded).

A Blissful Beach

The following morning, we emerged from our shady forest hideaway to discover it was sunny. So, we put Oslo on hold and went in search of a beach. We did some very sophisticated research, typing "beach near me" into Google. A beach near the village of Hydrostranda turned out to be a gem (///flattered.score.cuter).

We almost turned away because the site looked privately owned. We approached through a small holiday park, with smart chalets dotted on the hillside. The only member of staff we could find confirmed it was okay for us to park and use the beach for free, providing we didn't stay overnight. Deal.

The beach was in an idyllic cove - a small crescent of smooth white sand flanked by two outcrops of rock. There was only a handful of people there; some sun-bathing, others wading out into the shallow water with their kids. We spent a very relaxing couple of hours on the sands.

Refreshed, we drove a little further towards Oslo and stayed overnight in a beachside carpark just outside the quiet fishing village of Nevlunghavn (///dressy.unto.lengthen).

Oslo & The Weirdest Statues In The World

Driving into Oslo the next morning was a culture shock. It was our first big city visit since Stockholm. We struggled through the traffic, attempting to find camper parking near Frogner Park that had been recommended online. We caught glimpses of the parking area several times but couldn't get close to it. One-way road systems kept directing us out of the area, so we gave up. After a somewhat stressful search, we found on-street parking close to the southern end of Frogner Park (///stables.tonsils.squares). The Google lens app helped us decipher instructions on the parking meter and we paid £15 to stay for three hours.

The park attracts over a million visitors a year. Most go to see what one reviewer described as "The weirdest statues in the world". It's home to over two hundred statues created by Norway's most famous sculptor, Gustav Vigeland. His realistic, bronze and granite figures depict humanity – and not just the nice bits. Also, they all happen to be naked.

Many of the most striking figures stand on the parapets of a bridge. There's a man being attacked by three screaming babies.

It's a reflection on the challenges of fatherhood, apparently. We came face to face with 'Angry Boy'. His rage-filled features have become something of a Norwegian icon. At least, he appears on lots of postcards. There are countless other men, woman and children representing play, energy, and lust.

The most impressive single sculpture is a 14 m (46 ft) monolith. It features 121 intertwined figures, writhing and climbing over each other. They represent the various stages of life - children at the top - older men and women at the bottom. It took fourteen years to carve the monolith from a single piece of granite. Frogner Park is open all year and entry is free.

After returning to the van, we ran the gauntlet through Oslo city centre to the northern outskirts where we'd identified a vast car park where we could stay the night (///supporter.slipping.twins).

Capital Camping

Our stopover, close to a university campus, ticked lots of boxes. First, it was beside the Sognsvann metro station which had regular trains to the centre of Oslo on green line No 5.

Second, the car park bordered by a vast recreation area that includes Sognsvann Lake. We filled the evening strolling over two miles (3.2 km) around the lake's permitter. By the time we returned to the van, the car park was quiet. We settled down for the night with just a handful of other campers and trucks for company.

When we surfaced the next morning, the parking lot was already filling up again. Oslo's entire population seemed to be grabbing a jog, swim, or cycle ride in the park before heading off to work.

After breakfast, we walked the short distance to the nearby metro station and discovered there was no ticket machine. After downloading an app and buying a 24-hour pass (without too much difficulty for a change) we boarded a train for the city, where Steve had booked us a treat.

Floating Sauna

Our destination was Aker Brygge, a swanky commercial and tourist district in Oslo harbour. Formerly the site of an old shipyard, it's now a hugely popular complex of harbourside shops, bars, restaurants, and expensive-looking apartments. What *we* were looking for, was bobbing about in the harbour.

Norwegians are famously partial to their saunas. The hot steam element I understand. The plunging into ice chilly water follow-up has never had the slightest appeal.

There, at the bottom of a gangplank, was the KOK sauna (///harmony.jabs.husband). After a modest amount of sniggering, we walked down the gangplank onto a pontoon. A flotilla of small, square barges were attached to the floating platform with ropes. Each vessel had what looked like a chunky garden shed built on it. They were saunas. Floating saunas.

Closer inspection revealed each shed sauna had a ladder up to its flat roof - a space that could be used for socialising or jumping off if you fancied a swim in the harbour. Inside each cabin was a small, outer lobby for disrobing and a door leading through into the inner oven. We met the Sauna Master who introduced us to our barge, threw a few logs on the stove and left us to it.

The experience turned out to be even more relaxing than land-based slow cooking. As our temperatures soared, we were rocked gently - our sauna shed bobbing on the swell every time boats passed by.

Eventually, I was persuaded to attempt the obligatory cool-down in the harbour. Plunging in would almost certainly have resulted in cardiac arrest. So, I reversed, gingerly, down an aluminium ladder and, once my breathing re-started, enjoyed a short swim. My bravery evaporated when an enormous jellyfish pulsated by, and I scrambled back onboard.

Steve had pre-booked our session, guaranteeing we had a sauna to ourselves. It's cheaper to turn up without a reservation, but it may involve sharing your sauna space. We spent our entire session moored to the pontoon, but the barges are motorised, and there's the more expensive option to combine your sauna with a trip out to sea. The vessels are big enough for small sauna parties if that's your thing.

Session over, we got chatting to Sauna Master who was fascinated to hear about our adventure.

"It sounds like the road trip everyone would love to do, but never gets around to doing," he said.

It was good to be reminded how privileged we were, and we headed off to celebrate our good fortune with a beer. On the smart, busy dockside in Oslo, two pints of Kronenberg 1664 lager cost us an eye-watering £24. Yes folks - £12 a pint.

Our next destination was Oslo Opera House – not to catch a performance, but to climb on its roof. (///quarrel.playoffs.slab). This stunning, white building looks as though it has risen from the waters of the harbour. Its roof begins at ground level. We walked up its wide, gentle slopes to its highest point where we enjoyed spectacular views over the fjord and the city to mountains beyond.

Cool Salt

We rounded off our day in Oslo with a visit to SALT, one of the coolest destinations on the waterfront (///tapers.shield.womanly). It's a bit difficult to define. It's many activities take place in collection of buildings on a jetty in what feels like a more down-to-earth, working part of the harbour.

The SALT complex has six stages where you can enjoy comedy, concerts, films, and children's events. There are also six saunas, one of which can hold around a hundred people. We headed for SALT's street food vans which served a full range of international dishes. We enjoyed a tasty Mexican meal, paying much less than we feared, then took the metro back to the van for our second night in the Sognsvann car park - our final night in Norway.

18. THE ROAD TO GOTHENBURG

Having been somewhat blown away by Norway, the next country in our sights was Denmark. Every week there are around eighty ferry crossings on seven routes between the two countries. We weren't keen on spending around £200 for a 19-hour voyage from Oslo to Copenhagen, and besides, we had good reasons to go by road.

We opted to drive south down the western coast of Sweden so we could tick off two crucial destinations: the Saab car museum at Trollhättan, and the mighty bridge that links Malmo in Sweden with Copenhagen.

After leaving Oslo, we headed east on the E6 European route. We crossed the border into Sweden as we drove across the magnificent Svinesund Bridge. By lunchtime, we'd found a place to overnight; a free car park half way up a hill un an urban area, overlooking the town of Trollhättan and its mighty Got alv river. (///doped.worker.pictured).

A Roller Ski Invasion

Trollhättan is rarely on anyone's list of dream destinations - unless, like me, they need to pay homage at the spiritual home and birthplace of

Saab cars. But by chance, when we arrived for the weekend, so had over 1300 roller skiers from all parts of the globe.

We took an evening stroll along the clifftop paths that overlook the river and its usually spectacular waterfalls. The falls are the highest and most powerful in southern Sweden. They've been a tourist attraction since the 1700s and the site of the Olidan hydro-electric power station, where Sweden first attempted to produce electricity from waterpower in 1910. But when we turned up, all the water had gone. I suspect the flow had been diverted as there were major engineering works around the historic power station.

We ventured into the city which was largely deserted apart from its bars. They were over-flowing with exceptionally fit and cool-looking skiing types. You know, the type of people who wear sunglasses when it's dark. We decided we'd investigate more the next day, so dragged our exceedingly unfit selves back up the hill to the van and hit the sack.

The following morning, Trollhättan was manic. The main roads through the city had been closed off and were lined with spectators. There were giant TV screens, outside broadcast cameras and an outdoor TV studio. This roller ski business was clearly a much bigger deal than we'd realised.

A British roller-ski competitor overheard our Yorkshire accents and paused to chat. He said we had landed in the middle of world's biggest roller ski event. He explained that roller skiing is something top skiers do in the run up to the winter season. They clamp a cross between a short ski and a roller skate to their boots and use ski poles to propel themselves along the street. It's a way to build up their strength and stamina for the next skiing season; before there's any snow.

It was actually very exciting. Competitors reached astonishing speeds as they powered their way across the finish line. Crowds cheered. TV commentators got over-excited. We soaked up the atmosphere for a couple of hours before heading slightly out of town to a sacred site – The Saab Museum (///tides.migrate.shadows).

The Shrine Of The Saab

I won't go on about this, because I appreciate not everyone is as obsessed with Saabs as I am. Let's just say I've owned ten over the decades and am currently the custodian of a 32-year-old, bright yellow, much pampered Saab 900 Turbo convertible called Buttercup.

The museum showcases the slightly eccentric Swedish marque whose cars have a devoted following worldwide, but never seemed to earn the company enough money. Saab's rather bumpy road finally came to an end when it filed for bankruptcy in 2011.

Saab's heritage collection is in an old factory, not far from the company's original production plant. It displays cars and ground-breaking technologies from the company's birth in 1937 to its sad demise. There's an impressive array of Saab rally cars, including those driven by the legendary Erik Carlsson. Carlsson was born near Trollhättan and became the world's first rally-driving superstar, winning his first Monte Carlo rally in a Saab in 1962.

The museum also has as some truly stunning concept cars. Predictably, I loved it. But I'm sure anyone with an interest in cars, automotive technology or rallying would too.

After departing Saab city, we realised we were perilously close to running out of clean pants and headed towards Gothenburg in search of a campsite with a launderette. We ended up at Stenungsögården (///thaws.bunny.pointed) where we had a major washing session, made some calls home and did a spot of forward planning during a couple of day's break from the road.

An Overnight Challenge

Our next destination was Sweden's second biggest city, Gothenburg. I've mentioned how online reviews of stopover sites were one of the most useful features of our much-used camper apps. The Park4Night app translates reviews from all languages, includes a star rating and the date of the reviewer's visit.

We'd noticed a slightly disturbing theme to write-ups about several camper stops in and close to Gothenburg. Campervans and motorhomes were being broken into.

Throughout our trip, we had an un-written rule about the places we parked for the night. If a location made either of us feel the least bit uncomfortable, we'd move on and find another one. No arguments: no questions asked. But there was enough of a negative vibe about Gothenburg that we decided to find somewhere even further away from the city than we normally would. And wow, did we find somewhere.

It was close to the town of Surte, about 16 km (10 miles) north of the city. We climbed a hill through dense woodland into the Vättlefjäll nature reserve and found the car park in a clearing (/// bootleg.uniforms.toward). The parking is mostly for locals who take dips in the nearby swimming lake that we could see sparkling through the trees.

Nearby Surte offered two things we needed: a supermarket (a relief from Norway prices) and a railway station with free parking.

Gothenburg City

The following morning, we parked Cliff at Surte station (/// above.eminent.brief), downloaded another app to buy rail tickets, and took a twenty-minute train ride into Gothenburg Central – the oldest railway station in Sweden. Expanded and redeveloped in 1925, the building still has a 1920s feel with glass ceilings, wooden pillars, and limestone floors. It's a historic setting for a host of modern shops, bars, and restaurants, and well worth exploring even if you're not taking the train.

In front of the station, a mix of modern and rather ancient-looking trams depart for all corners of the city. But we set off on foot to explore nearby Trädgårdsföreningen, one of the best-preserved nineteenth century parks in Europe and an oasis of calm and colour in

Gothenburg's urban jungle (///fight.muddle.hedge).

The park is famed for its rose garden which boasts over twelve thousand varieties. But if your taste in plants is more for the weird and wonderful, don't miss the palm house (///footsteps.parks.tinkle). Opened in 1878, it's like a mini version of London's Crystal Palace. Each of its rooms has a unique climate, creating specific growing conditions for exotic and extraordinary plants from all over the world.

The park's also great for people-watching. We were intrigued by small group of unfeasibly flexible individuals. With no explanation of what they were doing, they took turns to bend their bodies into the most extraordinary positions we could imagine; as well as several we couldn't.

Food Hall Heaven

Somehow, the body benders didn't put us off lunch, so we made our way to Stora Saluhallen, Gothenburg's famous food hall, a ten-minute walk from the railway station (///foremost.canines.callers). The hall was opened in 1888 and still has a period feel. We wandered among independent food stalls selling the most mouth-watering array of Swedish produce.

Stallholders encouraged us to pull up a stool and taste their wares. But we opted to eat at one of the market's restaurants and tried traditional Swedish, open, prawn sandwiches. It was without doubt the freshest food we'd eaten in eight weeks.

There was huge potential for retail therapy in the city centre, but we gave it a miss. We'd been economically stretched by the prices in Norway and had no space to store souvenirs, even if we could afford them.

We made a quick visit to the harbour before catching the train back to Surte and returning to our woodland car park. We just managed to catch a dramatic sunset over the swimming lake.

After another peaceful night in the forest, we decided to make the most of our beautiful location. We spent two days doing nothing but visiting the beach and taking an occasional dip in the lake.

For nearly two months, we'd barely spent more than one night at each overnight location. Being constantly on the move is exciting but a never-ending stream of new experiences can cause a touch of unfamiliarity fatigue. It was good to take a break from driving and thinking and relax into our surroundings for a short while.

Running On Empty

When we finally decided to move on, our customary pre-flight checks revealed we were almost out of both diesel and LPG gas. We found diesel at an un-attended service station in Surte but were slightly baffled when all the diesel pumps had diagrams of trucks on them.

Hasty internet research re-assured us that 'truck' diesel is the same as any other. However, truck pumps have larger nozzles that don't fit cars. Cliff *could* accommodate the truck nozzle, as I assume, will most campers and motorhomes, as they're based on light commercial vehicles. Be aware that they dispense fuel a very high speed. Your tank can be full in seconds.

Finding LPG was a bigger challenge. Our Park4Night app wasn't showing many options – a bit of a surprise when we were close to a city the size of Gothenburg. We eventually found gas at a Preem filling station, but our search had taken us 25 miles (40 km) out of our way. We'd gone so far off course it wasn't practical to double back and visit Gothenburg's Volvo Museum as we'd planned. I was disappointed, but it renewed Steve's faith that there was a god.

Fully fuelled, we drove on to spend a couple of nights by a beach. Not a secluded cove this time, but a vast, deserted stretch of sand north of Varberg (///servant.pretend.eternal). The beach's official camper stop had toilets, an outdoor shower (no, of course we didn't) and waste facilities. There was everything we needed, plus glorious sands – all for free.

19. WONDERFUL COPENHAGEN

It was now September, and we were two months and 5,500 miles (8850 km) into our year-long adventure. We were heading towards Malmo, Sweden's third largest city, and the Swedish end of the spectacular Øresund Bridge.

A Celebrity Bridge

This bridge is famous. Not only is it the longest combined road and rail bridge in Europe, but it's also a TV star. We're big fans of 'Nordic noir'; films or TV shows, known for their dark storylines, deeply flawed characters, and oppressive atmospheres.

The Bridge TV crime drama starts when a dead body is discovered on the Oresund Bridge, right on the border line between Sweden and Denmark. Half of the deceased is in Danish territory – the other half is in Sweden. Detectives from both countries find themselves working together to track down the killer. There are countless other versions of the story acted out on borders throughout the world – including one about a corpse in The Channel Tunnel.

Obviously, we wanted some photos of the celebrity bridge. We pulled into a car park at an official viewpoint and found ourselves in the middle of a wedding (///wipe.prop.various). A bride, groom and various smartly dressed guests were posing by the waterside, determined to get the magnificent bridge in the background of their wedding photos. We loved Scandinavia's spectacular bridges – but not *that* much.

After the wedding party dispersed into the nearby conference centre, presumably for a reception, we walked along a boardwalk that protruded into Oresund sound – the waterway that separates Sweden from Denmark – and took our pictures.

Working out how to pay to cross the bridge took almost as much detective work as solving the fictional murder that took place on it. Online information was confusing, and we struggled with translations. First, we thought we needed to buy a pass in advance, but suspected they were for the many people who use the crossing on a regular basis, like those who work in Sweden but live in Denmark where property is cheaper.

Eventually, we drove onto the bridge without pre-booking and used a debit card to buy a one-way crossing from a toll booth. It was hassle-free and cost us £46.48.

We enjoyed driving on the vast structure for about five miles (8 km) before the roadway disappeared into hole. We hadn't realised that the bridge only stretches to Peberholmen, an artificial island. The carriageway then continues for a further two-and-a-half miles (4 km) in a tunnel before emerging in Denmark, just south of Copenhagen. Building the bridge all the way to the mainland would have created a hazard for planes using nearby Copenhagen airport.

A Giant Train Set

Our base for visiting the city was a car park, close to the Kastrup Street metro station on the M2 (Yellow) line that links the airport with the city centre (///juggler.definite.fellow).

Parking cost us £12 for our first night (Saturday). Our second night was free because there's no charge on Sundays. I've had fury-inducing experiences with car park apps in the UK, but the one we needed for this stay was simple to download, easy to use and extremely clever. If we left the car park early, it would refund any fees we hadn't used. If we needed to stay longer, we could open the app and pay more.

That Saturday afternoon, we intended to blow some of our wedding prezzie funds on a visit to Tivoli Gardens, one of the oldest theme parks in the world. The attraction inspired Walt Disney to create his Disney World resorts.

We crossed the car park to the metro station, bought 24-hour travel passes (about £9 each) and boarded the first train that pulled in. Unlike many capital city metro systems, Copenhagen's is relatively new. It's clean, silent, modern, and the train we boarded had no driver.

Back home, rail workers were striking because of plans to remove guards from some train services. Yet we were hurtling towards Copenhagen, plunging in and out of tunnels, and stopping at stations with no staff on board our train whatsoever. It was like riding a giant train set.

Theme parks are not my favourite things, but I'd thoroughly recommend visiting Tivoli (///parks.oaks.caller). The attraction opened in 1843 and is now close to the central station in the heart of the city; not that you'd notice once you're inside.

It's a blend of immaculate gardens, exotic buildings, and rides. There are nostalgic rides, good-old fashioned dodgems, and Ferris wheels. We loved its oldest and most popular attraction, a wooden rollercoaster that has been thrilling passengers since 1914. Each of its trains is still controlled by an eccentric brakeman who rides with you on board. It's all very quirky, rattly, and charming, but Tivoli has plenty for adrenalin junkies too. State-of-the-art white-knuckle rides weave in, around and over the more traditional attractions.

Tivoli is also great venue for foodies, offering much more than traditional hot-dog, ice-cream, and candy floss stalls. There are top-notch restaurants and a bustling food hall, which is where we headed for tea.

Our Tivoli tickets cost £70 each. That covered all rides and a meal with an alcoholic drink in the food hall. We had a tasty burger at 'Cocks and Cows' but could have used our vouchers at a range of French, Asian, Italian and Danish street food outlets.

We timed our visit to be in the park when it got dark. After nightfall, Tivoli takes on even more of a carnival atmosphere. The rides, stalls, restaurants, and even the flower beds are festooned in coloured lights. We rounded off our visit watching a show in Tivoli's open-air concert hall. Rock, jazz, pop, and opera concerts are held in this fairytale setting throughout the year.

The (Very) Little Mermaid

Next morning, we were up early and, again, took a driverless metro train into the city. I'd written a list of things to see and had attempted to group them efficiently around metro stations. Epic fail I'm afraid. There are only 22 stations on the Copenhagen metro system and the few that are in the city centre seemed very spaced out. So, we still ended up walking large distances and, thanks to my immaculate planning, frequently in the wrong direction.

We found The Royal Palace and after a stroll along the quayside found the iconic Nyhavn area (///harmony.jabs.husband). This canal-side street is famous for its coloured buildings and many restaurants. We even got to the Church of Our Saviour where you can climb its steeple via an outside staircase – if you've got the nerve (///envy.final.unhappy).

We also did what's expected of every visitor to Copenhagen – found our way to the iconic statue of 'The Little Mermaid' (///luring.ignoring.wipes). But she was not what I expected. I should have spotted the clue in her name. When you finally meet her in the flesh (bronze to be precise), she is surprisingly 'little' - just over four feet tall.

Ms Mermaid sits on a rock just off the Langelinie Pier. The poor creature is thronged. Tourists cram onto the pier to stare and take photos. Some climb down onto the rocks to grab selfies with her, despite signs warning them not to. On the water, a constant flow of harbour cruise boats motor up to her, bob about for a few minutes while their passengers take photos, then make way for the next in the queue.

The Little Mermaid statue was Inspired by Hans Christian Andersen's fairy story and has been a feature of the Copenhagen waterfront since 1913. Charming and popular though she undoubtedly is, the phrase we kept overhearing from many who battled through the crowds to catch a glimpse of her was "Oh, is that it!".

Kastrup Sea Bath

The following day, we decided to keep off the well-worn tourist trail and found a couple of truly alternative attractions. First, we drove a short distance from our overnight parking stop to the Kastrup Sea Bath. This wooden structure is in the sea, a few metres from the beach. It looks like a giant, wooden salad spinner floating in the water.

What happens there struck me as unusual. From the shore, people walk along a gangplank and enter the structure's inner sanctum where they're protected from the wind, and prying eyes, by its circular outer walls.

Once inside, they change into swimwear or dispense with clothes altogether. Then, they use make use of its 870 m (3000 ft) of decking to sunbathe or plunge into the deep seawater underneath the structure. We peeked inside, but as we had no intention of stripping off or throwing ourselves in the sea, we left far hardier souls to enjoy this uniquely Danish attraction. If you're tempted – it's free.

The Willy Wonka's Of Waste

Our next tourist attraction was also unconventional – a giant, award-winning, waste incinerator that produces heat and electricity for large parts of Copenhagen (///infects.stiff.bigger).

I appreciate that incinerators are usually something to avoid. But the Copenhill plant is a fascinating and surprisingly attractive addition to the Copenhagen skyline. From the outside, it's a rather beautiful building - a giant, aluminium wedge of a cheese grater. There's a slender chimney rising from its tallest end, releasing nothing nastier into the atmosphere than steam.

But it's what's on the steeply sloping roof that boggles the mind. There's a park, complete with a tree-lined hiking trail, a champagne bar and an artificial, 490 m (1600 ft) ski slope.

We decided to investigate and took a glass elevator from the visitor entrance up the inside of the building. It was like the Willy Wonka's of waste. From the lift, we could see some of the three hundred refuse trucks that dump rubbish at the plant every day. We got a bird's eye view of the furnaces and all the other techy gubbins that make it 'the cleanest waste-to-energy power plant in the world'.

Once on the roof, we soaked up the views of Copenhagen, then followed the ski-run which zigzags down the roof and turns around a corner of the building before sloping down one side to the ground. The outside of the building also features an almost 86 m (300 ft) climbing wall – said to be the tallest in the world. All these features are intended to make Copenhill an 'urban mountain' – an incinerator people want to visit rather than avoid.

20. HAMLET'S CASTLE AND COLD WAR CHILLS

One of my biggest challenges during our twenty country road trip was being hopeless at geography. Shamefully, before our adventure, I would have struggled to show you exactly where Denmark was on a map.

I'm now fairly sure where it is, and that it's made up of three main land masses. From left to right there's the tall narrow chunk that's connected to Germany. That's the Jutland peninsula. Then there are two main islands - the small Funen Island in the middle, and to the right, Zealand - the larger and most densely populated island which includes Copenhagen.

Having enjoyed exploring the capital city, we headed North to explore the rest of Zealand. Our first discovery was the Jægersborg Deer Park (///hitters.cars.resists). Its four square miles of parkland (11km^2) are home to over two thousand deer, said to be descendants of animals used centuries ago, by Danish royalty, for the very unpleasant purpose of 'par force' hunting.

This so-called sport involved chasing a stag with a pack of hounds until the poor creature was exhausted. Then someone, usually the Monarch, would put the animal out of its misery with a knife. The deer's meat was inedible due to the stress of the pursuit, so the animal was fed to the dogs. Traditionally, the hunter would keep the deer's right foreleg as a trophy. Nice.

King Christian V of Denmark was a huge fan of par force hunting, but presumably became less enthusiastic about it after a hunted stag gave him a severe kicking in 1698. The king's injuries are said to have contributed to his own death in the following year. Shame.

There's no hint of all that historical unpleasantness today. We spent a couple of hours wandering through the beautiful parkland and had reasonably close encounters with several herds of mostly fallow deer but also those of the red and sika varieties. It's a beautiful place to visit. Just try to forget what happened there in the past.

No Right To Roam

We had become a bit blasé about finding free places to overnight while travelling through Norway and Sweden, thanks to their generous laws on accessing the countryside. But there's no 'right to roam' in Denmark.

The land of the Danes is more densely populated than its Nordic neighbours and a greater proportion of its forests and countryside are privately owned. So, you can't just head into the Danish countryside and park for the night in any beauty spot you fancy. In Denmark, you must find locations where overnight parking is specifically allowed.

In practise, it's not as onerous as it sounds. We stayed in many car parks beside beaches and leisure areas or on the outskirts of villages and towns. They were either free or charged nominal fees. You're also allowed to park overnight in most lay-bys, or 'rasteplads' as the Danes call them.

However, to avoid any problems, it's important to look for and read any signs. Use the Google Lens app to translate if they're in Danish. Overnighting may be banned in specific car parks, or subject to local rules. We ended up being fined for parking in the wrong space in one car park because we didn't see the signage. More on that later.

Even in places where we *were* allowed to overnight, we had to treat it as parking, not camping. So, no awnings, camping chairs or barbeques, for example. In these spots, we made sure all our camping activities were inside the van.

Denmark does have over four hundred formal campsites that are suitable for campervans and motorhomes. But by now, we'd got out of the habit of using them.

That evening, we found a free car park sandwiched between the eastern edge of the Jægersborg Deer Park and the waters of Oresund sound, outside the village of Tarbaek (///think.choppy.octopus).

Louisiana Art Stop

Back in Copenhagen, two women we'd got chatting to in a bar had insisted that our visit to Denmark wouldn't be complete without a visit to a very quirky art gallery called 'Louisiana'. It didn't sound like our cup of tea, but the pair were insistent.

So, next morning, we drove north up the Zealand coastline and found the museum in a deceptively traditional looking 1870s villa (///astonishing.bureau.moguls). The next couple of hours boggled our minds... in a good way.

Behind Louisiana's rather strait-laced façade is a collection of modern art in a series of interconnected modern buildings, glass-walled passageways, subterranean galleries, and cinemas. The displays showcase over four thousand paintings, models, films, and sculptures from 1945 to the present day.

There are major works from the likes of David Hockney and Max Ernst. But there's nothing stuffy or pretentious about Louisiana. It's accessible, often baffling and frequently amusing.

Its sculpture park has statues by Henry Moore. But there's also an 8 m (26 ft) mobile swaying in the breeze – complete with a giant, bright-blue version of Big Bird from *Sesame Street* perching on a crescent moon.

And the name "Louisiana"? There's no connection with the North American state. The villa's original owner named it after his wives. They were called Louise. All three of them! The museum may be a bit "bonkers conkers", as my grandson would say, but it's well worth visiting if you fancy a decidedly different way to spend half a day.

Back at the van, we donated some of our Yorkshire teabag stash to a rather unprepared English couple we'd got chatting to in the sculpture park. They'd only been in Denmark for a few days but were already suffering from proper cuppa withdrawal symptoms.

With the day's good deed done, we drove on, almost to the northern tip of Zealand Island. We found a car park where overnights were allowed, close to the main road and overlooking the sound (/// husbands.wades.bother). We could see Sweden across the water, and south along our coastline, the magnificent silhouette of Hamlet's castle.

Hamlet's Castle

Generally, we don't make a point of visiting castles. Having walked around many, I'm currently at the 'seen one, seem them all' stage. But the castle that overlooks the northern opening to Oresund Sound is rather famous – so we thought it at least deserved an inspection.

The castle's real name is Kronborg – or the Crown Castle (/// detectable.tightening.clued). It's been a royal residence and a fortress, burned to the ground and re-built twice. It's now considered one of the most important Renaissance castles in Northern Europe and a UNESCO World Heritage Site. (See chapter main photo).

Most visitors are attracted by the castle's rather flimsy connection with Shakespeare. It's claimed The Bard based Hamlet's fictional 'Elsinore' castle on the real Kronborg which stands by the harbour at the real-life city of Helsingør. Elsinore; Helsingør… get it?

Shakespeare accurately described some unique features of the castle in his play about the Danish prince. However, there's no evidence he ever left England, let alone visited the northeast tip of Denmark. One explanation is that some of Shakespeare's acting troop *did* perform at the castle and told him about its magnificence when they returned home.

Today, 'Elsinore' makes the most of its Hamlet connections. The play is performed there on a regular basis. Actors Lawrence Olivier, John Gielgud, Derek Jacobi, and David Tennent have all been to the castle to star in the leading role.

We walked around the perimeter but opted out of exploring its impressive state rooms, vast ballroom, and creepy crypts. Instead, we climbed back into the van and headed back down Zealand Island.

Cold War Chills

After skirting around Copenhagen, we headed south-west. On Euro route 20, we saw several brown tourist signs advertising the "Panzermuseum East", so took a diversion to investigate (/// notebooks.brushed.jeering).

This museum, south-east of the city of Slagelse, turned out to be interesting but ever so slightly disturbing. It describes itself as Scandinavia's largest private collection of military vehicles from the Warsaw Pact. Essentially, it's all the hardware that would have been used to attack Denmark, or any other country for that matter, if the cold war had turned hot.

I'm a huge fan of Second World War History and have enjoyed wartime museums in England and France that bring great wartime stories to life. If they lift the lid on daring plots, ingenious inventions, and a spot of espionage, so much the better.

Perhaps TV and films have made the Second World War a little nostalgic for those of us fortunate enough not to have lived through the appalling reality of it. But this Cold War collection felt closer – more oppressive. Its exhibits are mostly tanks, armoured cars, radar equipment, helicopters, and planes. We were slightly taken aback to walk into one shed crammed with mobile, nuclear missile launchers – all safely de-militarised of course.

A sobering message had been hung on several of the collection's preserved tanks and armoured personnel carriers. It said examples of these vehicles were still being used by Ukrainian forces in their fight against the invading Russian Army.

I can't quite put my finger on why I felt a little uneasy about the collection. In fairness, its founder and owner is a self-confessed pacifist. He says it's a museum of "what could have been", and his aim is to educate, not glorify war.

We chose not to have a snack in "The Bomb Café", nor stay the night in museum's camping area. It was already filling up with wartime re-enactors ahead of an upcoming event. Instead, we overnighted in yet another free, waterside car park (///swung.squid.audition) with a distant view of our route off Zealand Island – The Great Belt Bridge.

21. ONWARDS TO ODENSE

Much to the annoyance of certain people, I'm usually up with the lark. But the next morning I was roused from my slumbers by a group of cars pulling into our car park. I heard people slamming doors and chatting excitedly, so I tweaked open the window blind to see what all the excitement was about.

Early Bird Bathers

I spied a group of senior citizens. Four of them were in fleecy dressing gowns. The fifth was a shamelessly naked man who was stood by the open boot of his car, struggling to hoist his swimming trunks. Once he'd gained control of his swimwear, he joined his pals. They walked to the water's edge, disrobed, threw themselves in the water and started to swim.

The early bird bathers had plunged into the Great Belt Straight, a stretch of water that's up to twenty miles (32 km) wide and lies between Denmark's Zealand and Funen islands. It effectively splits the country down the middle.

It was an overcast and slightly misty morning in the first week of

September. I'd barely had time to register how uninviting it all looked before the bathers emerged from the water. They gave no impression that their dip had been cut short by the cold. Still chatting and smiling, they dried themselves, put their dressing gowns back on and drove off.

I investigated this behaviour. There seems to be no scientific evidence that plunging your body into chilly water (often followed by a hot sauna) improves your health and wellbeing. However, those who partake are convinced that it does. In Denmark, 'sea dipping' is a year-round activity. Unaccountably, it's most popular in winter. The country has over ninety winter swimming clubs.

Did we test it out? Of course not. We had hot showers in our toasty, gas-heated campervan. By the time we'd downed a steaming coffee, the mist had cleared enough to give us a distant view of the magnificent Great Belt Bridge. After running through our customary pre-flight checks, we set off to drive across it (/// viewfinder.unify.clangs).

The Great Belt Bridge

Apologies about this, but I became really excited about yet another colossal bridge. The Great Belt Bridge is actually two bridges; an east and west bridge that use the small island of Sprogo as a kind of stepping stone across the water. Together, they're eleven miles (18 km) long. If you climbed more than eight hundred feet (254 m) to the top of the tallest bridge tower, you'd be at the highest point in the whole of Denmark.

The 'Great Belt Fixed Link', as it's also known, opened in 1998. It replaced a ferry service that had run since 1883 and, in its later days, took more than ninety minutes to cross the water. The bridge now forms part of the mighty E20 European highway – the only practical road connection between Scandinavia and the rest of Europe. Ok. Technically, there is an alternative route by road – but it involves driving through Russia.

Currently, there's a fee for making the Great Belt crossing. One way in our 6 m, sub-3.5 tonne campervan cost £22. That includes a discount because our bridge toll was collected by the automated EPASS24 system we'd signed up to. Standard pay-on-the-day fees at toll booths would have been about £32 for our van and an eye-watering £70 for a larger motorhome (over 6 m and over 3.5 tonnes).

However, a Danish campsite owner has gained widespread support for his campaign to have this crucial road connection made toll free. He's already forced the Danish parliament to discuss the issue. You can find the latest situation on tolls on bridge's website, https://storebaelt.dk

We didn't resent the toll. Apart from saving us a trip through Russia, crossing the monumental structure was a great experience. The mighty bridge finally deposited us safely on the smaller of Denmark's main islands, Funen.

We soon arrived in the city of Nyborg where we found an overnight parking spot, courtesy of our Park4Night camper app (/// digital.fussed.whoever). It was at a disused ferry terminal; presumably left redundant by the opening of the bridge we'd just crossed.

Rain had returned, so we busied ourselves booking tickets to a couple of exciting attractions for the days ahead. Our mood changed when a flurry of breaking news alerts pinged on our phones. Back home, various members of The Royal Family were rushing to Balmoral following a deterioration in The Queen's health.

I appreciate this is ridiculous but, bear in mind, we had been away from Blighty for almost nine weeks by this time. I'm also fully aware that our presence in England would not have made the slightest difference to unfolding global events. But that afternoon, wandering through Nyborg, we were subdued and had a very peculiar feeling that we should have been at home.

Hi-Tech Fairy Tales

The next morning, we lightened the mood with a short drive to the city of Odense. We were on the trail of the famous Danish children's author, Hans Christian Andersen. I was worried this visit might end up being filed under 'rather obvious and well-worn' tourist destinations; but not a bit of it.

We rocked up at the new Hans Christian Andersen House (///hydrant.reinforce.cloud). Opened in 2021, this development of state-of-the-art buildings uses the latest tech to bring the Danish hero and his fairy stories to life.

Twelve international artists helped to develop the project which is more immersive experience than museum. English language headsets accompanied us from one magical space to another, with friendly old Hans dropping a cheerful commentary in our ears.

Usually, I end up wanting to rip audio guides off my head and stamp on them. They never seem to marry up with what I'm looking at. But here, the tech was flawless. Individual exhibits trigger their own audio when you approach them. Our movements cued lighting changes, music, voices, and animations. It was all brilliantly done.

Kids of all ages will love the museum because it features all H.C.A.'s top tales: The Ugly Duckling; The Princess and the Pea; Thumbelina; The Little Match Girl and, of course, The Little Mermaid. But it also reveals the man behind the fairy stories. Through his letters and diaries, Andersen shares his struggle to escape childhood poverty and his distress when he couldn't get anyone to publish his work. There are intriguing insights into Andersen's private life. He fell hopelessly in love many times, but none of his relationships was successful.

In short, Hands Christian Andersen Hus is well worth a visit, however old you are. I need to include one footnote to avoid confusion. Odense has several attractions associated with its most famous son. The Hans Christian Andersen Birthplace House is beside the modern museum we visited. You can look around it with the same entrance ticket. It's not to be confused with the author's 'Childhood Home' – a more traditional and separate museum in the city's old town (///braced.beard.trailer).

The Little Belt Bridge

From Odense, we continued west across Funen Island on the E20, but took a detour to visit yet another bridge. Don't yawn. This is not a bridge too far; you can walk right over the top of this one.

Work started on the original Little Belt Bridge in 1925. Ten years and two million rivets later, it opening to form the first ever link between Funen Island and Jutland. The bridge was so ambitious in its day, it became a tourist destination while it was being built.

Today, it has a visitor centre where you can join up to twenty other folks on a two-hour bridge walking experience. You're provided with overalls to wear over your own clothes. Once you're tethered to the safety rail, you'll climb sixty metres up into the bridge structure, with spectacular views over the Little Belt Straight and Funen. Or at least, that's what the website and reviews suggest. We'd just missed the last climb of the day so couldn't make the ascent. Top tip: If you fancy bridge walking, book in advance to avoid disappointment. https://bridgewalking.dk/en/

By the 1950s, the boom in car travel had already turned the bridge into a bottleneck and its larger replacement, the *New* Little Belt Bridge, was opened in 1970.

That night, we parked a short distance from the original bridge at Fænø Odde Rasteplads (///fishing.evolves.willpower) - an official camper stop that overlooks the Little Belt Straight. The site was almost full of campervans and motorhomes when we arrived. We squeezed into one of the last available spaces, enjoyed watching what looked like sea lions frolicking some distance across the water. They were too far out to be sure. We settled down for the night, blissfully unaware that we were breaking the law.

22. LEGO®TOWN JOYS AND A TASTE OF THE SAHARA

During the night, someone had sneaked up to our camper and stuck a parking ticket on the windscreen. We had inadvertently parked in a bay that should not be used for overnight stays. The campervan right beside us had parked legally but had masked the sign that would have warned us against committing such a heinous crime. We should have looked harder. Later, we appealed, pleaded English ignorance, blamed the Dane's inadequate signage, but still ended up paying a fine of £60.

That morning, however, we couldn't be incandescent with rage for long. We had tickets for the LEGO® House. We re-joined the E20 and drove over the New Little Belt Bridge - our toll-free crossing to the Jutland peninsula and on to Billund, or LEGO® town as it should be called.

Lego® House

The public car park next to LEGO® House has height restrictions, so we parked CLIFF at Granjev 9 (///vows.nuance.koala) a designated car park for the attraction that has a handful of larger spaces for campervans and motorhomes. After a fifteen-minute walk into town, we arrived at the LEGO® company's newest attraction (/// dragons.talking.grid).

Cards on the table time. We both love LEGO®. I spent my entire childhood irritating my parents by endlessly scraping around for bricks in a metal tin. Somewhat later life, I confess to collecting some of the vintage 1960s and 70s LEGO® trucks I had when I was a kid. Steve and I even had a LEGO® construction site wedding cake. This was never going to be anything but a fantastic day.

Like most things in the LEGO®verse, LEGO® House is great for kids – but not *just* for kids. It's an exciting blend of modern museum, exhibition spaces and interactive experience zones spread over several floors – all containing over twenty-five million LEGO® bricks.

We started at the bottom in the basement museum. It tells the entire LEGO® story through examples of its products, starting with the wooden toys created by company founder Ole Kirk Christiansen in 1932. Christiansen set up his business only a few miles from where LEGO® House stands today.

Displays cover the monumentally important development and patenting of the first interlocking plastic brick – an invention the company protects very carefully. Some discarded moulds used to create bricks are sealed in concrete under the LEGO® House floor, to stop them falling into the wrong hands.

The ups and downs of the company are told through examples of LEGO® toys and sets from each year. The museum acknowledges the times when it struggled to survive; overcoming economic challenges and responding to huge shifts in the way children play with toys.

The middle floors are packed with a whole series of giant LEGO® layouts - plastic fantastic cityscapes, modelled in unbelievable detail. They switch from day to night-time mode. Volcanos explode. Trains run in and out of mountain tunnels. Street scenes bustle with pedestrians, cars, and buses. Close by, there were interactive games and challenges for kids, using real or virtual LEGO® bricks.

We thought the most impressive model was the 15 m (50 ft) 'Tree of Creativity'. It's made of over six million bricks and took over 24,000 staff hours to build. A stairway takes you up through the branches of the tree as you explore the building.

The top floor houses 'The Masterpiece Gallery' – an exhibition space for models and sculptures made by adult LEGO® superfans all over the world. Three enormous dinosaurs held centre stage when we visited, though the exhibition is constantly changing as amateur designers produce even more impressive creations – presumably audition pieces for coveted jobs as LEGO® designers.

Our most unforgettable experience was being served lunch by LEGO® robots Robert and Roberta. As we took our pre-booked seats in one of the Lego®House restaurants, we were handed a small bag of LEGO® bricks. Each brick corresponded to an item of food on the menu. That's because the LEGO® Mini Chefs, who would make our meals in the kitchen, don't understand written words; they only understand bricks. Fair enough.

Like a couple of excited six-year-olds, we made our menu choices, clicked the corresponding bricks to a LEGO® board and inserted it into a computer terminal on our table.

A video screen lit up and displayed what was happening to our order in the kitchen. An army of Mini Chefs deciphered our order and prepared our food. Ok, we were watching animations – but I'm sure they were tailored to exactly what we'd ordered.

When our meals were ready, we saw the chefs pack our food into LEGO® boxes on wheels and place them on railway tracks. Seconds later, the boxes appeared in real life on tracks suspended from the restaurant ceiling and spiralled down until they landed in front of Robert and Roberta.

After a great deal of enthusiastic robo arm waving, the animatronic waiting team lifted our boxes from the conveyor and handed us our food. It was great fun, and the food was surprisingly good too.

That evening, we stayed at the nearby LEGOLAND® Holiday Village (///reared.rudeness.negotiates) just across the road from LEGOLAND®. The village has generous capacity for campervans and motorhomes, its own restaurant, takeaway, supermarket, laundry, and mini golf.

Legoland® At Last

The next morning, my childhood dream of visiting the proper LEGOLAND® (i.e., not the UK version) finally came true (///unionists.untroubled.obediently). I'd been a tad concerned when I discovered, only recently, that the LEGO® hasn't owned the attraction for nearly twenty years. The brickmeisters sold off their theme parks in 2005 during financial difficulties.

Today, LEGOLAND® has all the white-knuckle and child-friendly rides you'd see at most theme parks. But, thankfully, LEGO® attractions are still its focus, including Miniland – the giant model village that's been at the core of the park since it opened in 1968.

It's the place to discover the world in 1:20 scale; everything from capital cities to the tallest buildings – all created with over twenty million bricks. There are iconic Danish scenes that that have been miniaturised in plastic for decades.

On balance, I reckon LEGO® House offers the purest experience for folks obsessed with the brick. LEGOLAND® still ticks plenty of LEGO® boxes but is probably the better bet for an all-round family day out.

Next morning – a Monday in mid-September – we drove out of Billund past LEGOLAND® and the resort was closed. Top Tip: if you are visiting any attractions in Scandinavia, always double check when they are going to be open. Opening days and times vary enormously depending on the season. We missed out on visiting several smaller venues because they either opened at weekends only – or, once August and the school summer holidays were over, shut down for the winter season. I assume it's because Scandinavia doesn't have the population, visitor numbers or the weather to justify attractions being open all year round.

We dedicated our next day to driving, determined to get as far north up the Jutland peninsula as we could. After the brightness and busyness of Billund, the countryside felt deserted.

There were plenty of campsites but having spent the previous two nights in a 'resort' we fancied some budget-stretching peace and quiet in a beach-side car park. We found one down a rough track near Dronninglund (///mozzarella.password.leave). After a bracing walk across the sand dunes, we settled down for the night.

It was another night where the rain clattered on the van roof. We'd come to like it. However, next morning, barely awake, I opened Cliff's sliding side door to discover we were surrounded by water. If a scene from *Chitty Chitty Bang Bang* comes to mind – the one where Chitty magically transforms into a boat - it was just like that.

At first, I thought the tide had come in, but the sea was still some distance away beyond the sand dunes. A good deal of the previous night's rain had drained to our end of the car park, and we were in the middle of a giant puddle. Luckily, it was only about 20 cm (8 ins) deep – not enough to float us away while we'd slept.

Our next destination was considerably drier. In fact, it was as though we had been teleported to the Sahara Desert.

A Taste Of The Sahara

We made our way to the Råbjerg Mile Sand Dune. Forget the discreet little dunes you get at the edge of a beach. This one is a whopper. It's roughly two-thirds of a mile (1 km) square and over 40 m (130 ft) high. We parked Cliff on one of the few roads that lead to the dune (///assertions.closer.frosty) and set off to explore the giant heap of sand.

Climbing a massive sand dune in the north of Denmark is a surreal experience. Once you're on it, the undulating terrain and high ridges mean all you can see is sand. The wind catches tiny particles and sand blasts your face. You really could be in a desert; in a scene from *Star Wars;* or on Mars.

It's estimated the Råbjerg Dune contains over 3.5 million cubic metres (120 million cubic feet) of sand. But what's more staggering, is that the giant sand mass is on the move – and has been for centuries. Each year, it creeps about 15 m (50 ft) in a north-westerly direction towards the top of Jutland. To put this in context, if we'd parked Cliff at the front edge of the dune, it would be forty years before the sands passed over him and he re-appeared behind it.

Having substantial amounts of sand blowing around this part of Denmark has its challenges. Entire villages have been buried. Just south-west of Skagen, we visited the remains of a church that was half buried by sands from nearby dunes (///adored.handing.mastermind).

In the eighteenth century, stoic parishioners refused to give up on their place of worship, digging their way in through the entrance each time they want to hold a service. Eventually, they gave up and the church was closed in 1795.

Having read about the church online, we got the impression we would be able to explore a buried church. We couldn't. Most of the building was demolished. All that's left now is the top of the tower, sticking out of the… sand.

Where Two Seas Collide

As if a giant sand dune wasn't enough, we still had another natural phenomenon to tick off our list. We drove a little beyond Skagen, Denmark's most northerly town, until the road ended in a large car park where we would stay the night (///fudged.transpiring.gown).

We had reached Grenen, the top of mainland Denmark. Here, a thin, spindly finger of land points north from the top of the Jutland peninsula. On foot, we followed a well-signed path over more sand dunes towards the fingertip, a truly remarkable headland.

We stood on the outcrop of sand with the sea on either side of us. The sandy strip stretched into the distance, eventually narrowing, and disappearing under the waves - waves that mess with your head.

I have lived by the sea. My brain knows that waves all travel in the same direction, usually towards or away from you, parallel to the beach. But something quite different happens at Grenen. It's the place where two seas collide.

As you look north along the sand bar, waves originally from the Baltic Sea crash in from the right and breakers from the North Sea pile in from the left. Both sets of waves collide in a straight line that stretches far out into the distance. It's hard to compute what you're looking at.

The scene is even more spellbinding because the opposing waves smash into each other with such force. There's strictly no swimming at Grenen because the currents at this spellbinding location are always too strong.

We were transfixed by the spectacle until it began to get dark and the tide (correction; tides) threatened to cut us off from the mainland.

We walked a mile or so (1.5 km) back to the car park. During the day, there is the option of taking the 'sandworm' to Grenen. It looks like a railway carriage towed by a tractor. The service usually runs between 10 am and 4 pm, but with no fixed timetable.

Parking and staying overnight was free when visited. However, charges apply during June, July, and August.

23. OLD TOWN RIBE AND A BRAND-NEW BEACH

We felt a little deflated when we drove away from Grenen. Heading back from Denmark's most northerly point meant we were technically on our way home - even if it was a temporary measure. But we still had some great locations on our 'must do in Denmark' list.

After a long day's driving, we made it more than half-way down Jutland's west coast to the city of Esbjerg. We found a spot to overnight in a harbourside car park close to a lightship - a kind of floating lighthouse that was built in 1914 and is now a museum (/// vision.stumpy.lobby).

Esbjerg is Denmark's largest fishing port and home to many businesses that support the offshore oil and gas industry. It felt a little bleak and industrial – not helped by the black cloud that had been following us around, hovering above Cliff as though he was that creepy hearse in the old Wacky Races cartoons.

Celebrating The Sea

It's claimed that wherever you go in Denmark, you are never more than about thirty miles (50 km) from the sea. I suppose that makes sense in a country that is made up of over 1400 islands and has over 4,500 miles (7,300 km) of coastline.

Denmark celebrates its connection with the sea at the Fisheries and Maritime Museum in Esbjerg. We arrived too late in the afternoon to visit the attraction, so missed its aquarium, sealarium (home to resident sea lions) and 'Mysteries of the Sea' exhibition which, apparently includes giant whale hearts, a mermaid skeleton, and the gruesome tale of a giant squid.

Next morning, however, the weather was much improved, and we were able to visit what had drawn us to Esbjerg in the first place. "Man Meets the Sea" is a giant monument that's close to the fisheries museum (///point.caged.bashful). Four concrete men sit, side-by-side, staring across Saeding Beach and the entrance to Esbjerg harbour. They're pure white, 9 m (37 ft) tall, with ramrod straight backs and no expression whatsoever. They could be statues from an ancient temple who have taken a break by the Danish seaside. They could also pass as Dr Who villains, silently contemplating the destruction of the planet. I'm getting carried away. But these majestic and eerie figures are well worth a visit. There's a picnic area and car park close by.

Good Old Ribe

While Esbjerg is one of Denmark's newest cities, a 45-minute drive south took us to its oldest town, Ribe. After parking for free beside the railway station (///slug.sweltering.flop), we walked into Ribe's historic centre. It's a pretty town with cobbled streets, half-timbered houses and no shortage of coffee bars, souvenir shops and small galleries.

Ribe's centrepiece is the Our Lady Maria cathedral (///strategist.developed.line). It's believed Denmark's first Christian church was built on the site in the Viking era. Archaeologists have discovered Viking burials, but no sign of an original wooden church. The building you see today was built in the 12th and 13th centuries.

The cathedral suffered a major fire in 1176 and on Christmas morning 1283, of all days, its north-west tower collapsed, killing many worshippers. Climbing one of the present-day towers gives you magnificent views over Ribe and the surrounding countryside.

After a pleasant mooch around the central shopping area, we returned to the van and headed off for our final overnight location in Denmark – a picnic spot south-west of Tønder, close to the German border (///buns.infamous.earrings).

We were 6,500 miles (10,460 km) into the first leg of our year-long adventure. However, for very irksome reasons I'll explain later, our welcome in Europe was about to run out. We had only two weeks left before we had to catch a ferry home and continue at least part of our road trip in the UK.

Next morning, we crossed into Germany and drove through torrential rain for nearly two hours before arriving at Campingplatz zur Perle (///soft.clammed.formulas) - a then very soggy campsite at the coastal town of Büsum. It was the first official campsite we'd booked into for some time. Remember, the Germans don't take kindly to campers overnighting anywhere but designated stopover sites.

Büsum Buddies

Büsum is a popular seaside playground for the residents of Hamburg, a ninety-minute drive away. Officially, 99.5 per cent of the visitors to this resort and spa town are German. Feeling distinctly outnumbered, we braved the drizzle and took a short walk through the campsite towards the sea.

For hundreds of years, Büsum suffered severe flooding and much of the town is now on land reclaimed from the sea. We climbed to the top of a giant flood barrier which runs along the shoreline and had our first view on an artificial island and beachfront called Perlebucht.

This smart, new complex was designed to provide the perfect day at the beach. For families, there are beach bars, play areas, picnics spots, barbeque points, hammocks, and beach chairs inside individual box-like shelters. One attraction is a huge draw for water sports enthusiasts – an artificial lagoon between the created island and the mainland that's not affected by the waves or tides.

That afternoon, the lagoon was swarming with kitesurfers making the most of its smooth waters and the brisk winds. These excessively athletic individuals spent most of their time making spectacular jumps into the air. Once airborne, they hung from their flimsy canopies and somehow had enough time to detach their surfboards from their feet, wave them around and fastened them back on again – presumably for no other reason than they could.

If you're serious about trying water sports in Büsum, first, be very careful how you search for such activities online. Eventually you should discover schools for kitesurfing, windsurfing, and wing foiling.

Our second day in Büsum was a weather write-off. In nearly three months on the road, it was the first time that rain had confined us to the van for the entire day. Over the following 48 hours, we continued west towards the Netherlands. We spent a couple of nights at *Camping Hümmlinger Land* campsite in Lower Saxony (/// remembering.blogs.recovered). We felt we should settle somewhere to watch live coverage of the Queen's funeral.

The next day, we crossed the border into Holland and superb Dutch roads helped make it a quick and pleasant journey to Strandpark Vlugtenburg, just north of the Hook of Holland (/// antisocial.freezers.backrest). It's the campsite we'd used on the first night of our adventure. But we weren't ready to board the ferry just yet.

24. ROTTERDAM REVELATIONS

I can't pretend Rotterdam was on my list of 'must-see' destinations. I'd never thought of it as anything more than a giant container port. But our visit to the city proved just how wrong I could be.

Our first mission was to find a parking spot on the outskirts of the city that was big enough for Cliff, and close enough to a metro line that could whizz us into the centre. Once again, the Steve/Park4Night app partnership triumphed, and we found a beautiful spot in Schiedam, one of Rotterdam's eastern suburbs (///acid.slower.pastels).

Our space was beside a picturesque canal and close to one of eight old windmills that are dotted around the city. Schiedam once had twenty such mills that ground grain for the gin-making process – a local speciality.

It was an extremely attractive location, but we'd seen some confusion online about whether campers could stay there overnight. I can confirm there were six parking spaces designated for campers. From what we could translate, it looked as though an overnight stay would have been free, but there were parking charges during the day.

Overnight parking facilities are rare in The Netherlands, particularly in urban areas. Confusingly – and probably the cause of the online debate – the Schiedam location had a sign declaring "Camping behaviour not allowed". We took this to mean a rule we had become familiar with on our travels; that *parking* overnight is fine, but you're not allowed to do any activity outside your van that looks like camping.

We paid for our parking and made our way to the ultra-modern, un-manned Parkweg underground station nearby (/// falters.bothered.obey). It's possible there may have been some cursing and swearing as we struggled to extract train tickets from the machine. Eventually, we took a twenty-minute journey along the red line to Eendrachtsplein, one stop short of Rotterdam city centre (/// supplied.pockets.frogs).

Lost Art In A Salad Bowl

It was the closest metro station to "The Depot" (/// fingernails.potions.option) – an extraordinary building we'd first seen on a TV travel show before we left home. In the flesh, it looks like a 40 m (130 ft), seven storey, stainless steel salad bowl. One of its architects was said to have been inspired by a four €4 IKEA salad bowl during a meeting to brainstorm designs.

This recent addition to the Rotterdam skyline is a striking and expensive (€90 million) art storage facility. The nearby Boijmans Van Beuningen Museum has been collecting art for over 170 years, but like many similar institutions, has space to display only a fraction of its posessions.

So, 150,000 of the main museum's items that were once stored away from public view can now been seen in The Depot. But don't mistake it for an overflow museum. There are no exhibitions or conventional galleries. None of the items are arranged in chronological order or themes. Instead, objects are stored on shelves or racks in which of many storage compartments has the best climatic conditions to preserve them.

The building would be worth a visit even if it were empty. Its core is open, with criss-crossing escalators and walkways taking you to all floors. The sheer randomness of the exhibits (sorry, stored items) makes it continually surprising. One minute, we were close-up with a priceless Van Gough painting, the next trying to get our heads around an old-fashioned telephone with a receiver made from a plastic lobster. There's art and objects from the 1200s to the present day – just not in any particular order.

If you don't suffer from vertigo, head for the roof where there's smart restaurant and gardens with magnificent views of the city.

Rotterdam Food Hall

Our next stop was another spectacular building – Rotterdam's food hall (///lace.jogging.multiple). It's a mecca for foodies and the largest indoor market in The Netherlands. You could mistake it for a giant, horseshoe shaped aircraft hangar with giant glass windows at each end. Inside, there are over one hundred food stalls, fifteen shops and eight restaurants in an area the size of a football pitch.

While the fresh produce on display is mouth-watering, the most striking thing about the building is its 40 m (130 ft) high, curved ceiling. It's 'The Horn of Plenty' - an enormous, psychedelic artwork, painted on over four thousand giant tiles. It's a cornucopia of fish, fruit, flowers, and vegetables and claimed to be the biggest single artwork in the world.

Somehow, the walls of the food hall building contain 288 apartments and its basement houses a four-storey car park. Just when we thought The Dutch couldn't be more inventive with buildings, a short walk beyond the food hall brought us to completely crazy housing development (///apple.tablet.handed).

Living In A (Tilted) Box

The Cube Houses must be the most impractical homes on the planet. They're cube-shaped – obviously. Each box-like dwelling stands on a concrete pillar and is tilted at an angle of 45 degrees. (See chapter main photo). There isn't one vertical wall inside them. Some of their windows point into the sky, others towards the ground.

These wonky, yellow and white houses were designed in the late 1970s by the Dutch architect Piet Blom. His concept was that each house represented a tree. Together, they form an urban forest. That's all very marvellous, but if you lived in one, how would you put a shelf up?

The cube houses are one of Rotterdam's main tourist attractions, but they're not a gimmick. They *are* occupied. One property is kept as a museum, so you can get a glimpse of what it would be like to live inside a slanted box.

Overall, Rotterdam felt vibrant and well worth considering for a city break or long weekend. Certainly a refreshing alternative to the rather obvious attractions of Amsterdam. But our time in the Netherlands was almost up. We took the metro back to Schiedam and managed a quick look around the charming old town before driving Cliff back to our campsite. There was only one problem; we couldn't get in.

The camera at the automatic entrance gate didn't recognise our numberplate. The barrier refused to budge even though we drove up to it several times. Someone (probably me) had thrown away the campsite's out-of-hours telephone number, so we had to wait until we found someone who'd had the sense to keep theirs. Two Top Tips: don't trust technology and don't bin campsite contact numbers until you depart.

Heading Home (For Now)

Our next move takes some explaining. After travelling for three months, we were in the swing of life on the road. We'd adjusted to living in our own (non-tilted) box on wheels. We'd finally developed a form of muscle memory for moving around the confines of our campervan. The scars caused by repeatedly banging my head were finally starting to heal.

We'd fallen into a routine for cooking, cleaning, topping up LPG and scheduling laundry stops. We'd cracked visiting cities and big attractions. We'd even braved overnighting in the wilderness, where permitted, and now thought nothing of it.

In an ideal world, we would have followed the sun and spent the winter in southern Spain. This was certainly our plan when we first envisaged our trip some years earlier.

However, because of Brexit, we were no longer allowed to do that. Three months into our grand adventure, we had to temporarily return to the UK. Our ferry back to Harwich was booked for the next day.

The Brexit Effect

Since the UK parted company with the European Union, we Brits are no longer European citizens. This means we've lost our rights to travel wherever we like in the EU for as long as we fancy.

Our movement is now restricted. The rules on how, where and for how long we can travel are annoyingly complicated. I've attempted to make sense of them in my previous advice-based book *Europe by Campervan* and on my Vanlife Virgins blog (www.campervanvirgins.com).

In a nutshell, we Brits are not allowed to travel in countries that are part of the so-called 'Schengen Zone' for more than 90 days in any consecutive 180-day period. In our case, by the end of September, we'd been in Schengen countries for nearly three months and were within days of using up our 90-day allowance. We had to get out of the zone, or potentially face fines or deportation!

The UK is not in the EU or the Schengen area, so is unaffected by the rules. We were going to use the UK as a bolthole. Spending 90 days back home would re-set our travel day allowance. After that, we could resume our adventures overseas.

As we drove onto our ferry at the Hook of Holland, I can't deny it felt odd to be heading back to the UK. We couldn't go 'home' home because we still had a tenant in our flat. We'd be spending October, November, and December living fulltime in our van – a period when most UK campervans and motorhomes are in hibernation.

We had become accustomed to stretching our travel budget by camping off grid – but knew we'd land in deep doo-doo if we attempted anything like that in England.

But there was still plenty to be positive about. Our plan was to tick off many UK destinations that we'd always fancied but never managed to visit. We'd enjoy Scotland's incredible NC500 route at a time of year when it wasn't swarming with midges or other campervans.

We'd also be around for a family wedding, the birth of a grandson and a big birthday bash. But most of all, it gave us time to plan.

Still To Come...

The next overseas leg of our adventure would eventually take us through twelve more countries. We'd travel south through France and Spain to the Rock of Gibraltar. We'd explore the delights of the Mediterranean coast, grab a glimpse of the high life in Monte Carlo and tick off some truly spectacular bucket list destinations in Italy.

And further down the line, those pesky post-Brexit travel rules would result in an unexpected bonus, forcing us to be even more adventurous on our travels.

As you'll see in future books in this series, we'd end up exploring Albania, North Macedonia, Montenegro, and Slovenia – truly amazing countries that had never been on our radar, let alone part of our big fat campervan road trip plan.

◆ ◆ ◆

Footnote:
If you've enjoyed part one of our European road trip - there's more to come. To receive notifications when future books are published, sign up to my Vanlife Virgins blog - at: https://www.vanlifevirgins.com/contact-vanlife-virgins/

APPENDIX 1

What3words - and how to use it:

The clever folks at 'what3words' have divided the entire globe into three metre squares and given each square a unique identifier made up of three words. They're as accurate as GPS co-ordinates, but a whole lot simpler than endless strings of numbers. Once you have the three magic words, you can find any location on the planet, and tell the maps or navigation devices on your phone to take you there.

Throughout this book, I've shared over 150 what3words locations for places we've stopped, parked and camped. Here's how you can find those locations for yourself:

1) Download the free 'what3words' app onto your mobile device

2) Type in the three words of the location you're looking for. Take care when typing. Adding just one wrong letter could take you to entirely the wrong location! And don't forget the full stops between each word.

3) The app may offer several location options. Click on the correct one. You'll then see the location on a map, or you can choose a satellite view.

4) Click "Navigate" at the bottom of your screen and select whichever navigation tool you use. The location will then become the destination in your navigation device.

We'd like to thank what3words for permission to feature their useful and ingenious invention in this book.

WITH THANKS...

to 'what3words' for permission to feature their ingenious, location pin-pointing system throughout this book...

to the talented Ellie Lewis for illustrating the cover...

and to top travelling companion and Hubster Steve, whose tireless location research made our once-in-a-lifetime trip spectacular and led to many of the unforgettable experiences shared in this book.

ABOUT THE AUTHOR

Chris Wise

It's not long since Chris Wise was a vanlife virgin. But he's just back from an epic campervanning adventure - a year-long, 21,000-mile road trip through Europe in a Fiat campervan called Cliff.

Chris's books follow his personal campervanning journey - from being bitten by the bug hiring a classic VW splitty campervan, through having a VW T6 Transporter converted into his first camper, to his amazing grown-up gap year exploring twenty countries.

As a journalist and TV producer, Chris's previous life included producing current affairs documentaries, lifestyle series including ITV's This Morning, and hundreds of programmes for the Discovery Networks.

Chris now splits his time between writing, producing videos for the NHS and 'The Campervan Channel' on YouTube. He lives in campervanning heaven - York - sandwiched between the spectacular Yorkshire Moors and Dales, with his Hubster and travelling companion, Steve.

BOOKS BY THIS AUTHOR

Europe By Campervan

Do you dream of making an epic campervan road trip, but need help to make it happen?

"Europe by Campervan" is packed with top tips, inspiration, and information to help turn your vanlife vision into reality.

It's everything the author wishes he'd known before he set off on a year-long, 21,000 mile campervan road trip through twenty European countries (including England and Scotland) – on a budget of just £60 for two people per day!

It's a friendly, first-timer's guide, covering:

* Motorhome or campervan – which is best for your big adventure?
* Wild camping in a motorhome or camper – where you can park for free in Europe and not break the law
* Schengen area rules – the challenge of post-Brexit travel restrictions for Brits on big trips
* Travel Tech – apps, gizmos and gadgets to make life easier travelling in a van
* Safety and Security – protecting you and your van while you're on the road
* Driving essentials – the lowdown on campervan insurance, green cards and road tolls
* Van life UK – the rules, regulations, and opportunities of exploring closer to home, including wild camping in Scotland, budget-busting pub stopovers and tackling the legendary NC500.

As the author says: "We would never have believed we were the sort of people who would do this. But we came up with a way to put our lives and work for the NHS on hold and just decided - let's do it. If this book does anything, I hope in inspires wannabe road trippers to start planning and believing their adventure can happen."

Vw Campers For Beginners

You know you need a VW camper. The only question is how are you going to get one?

"VW Campers for Beginners" is the essential guide for anyone wanting to turn their campervan dreams into reality.

It's packed with top tips, practical hints and useful checklists for anyone thinking of having a van converted or buying a ready-made camper.

It's a friendly, non-nerdy guide, based on the author's first-time experience of buying a T6 panel van and handing it over to a professional converter.

But there's expert advice too. VW specialists highlight do's, don'ts and common mistakes to help you save time and money and avoid potential pitfalls.

And if you're besotted with classic VW campers, there's a buying guide to these characterful campervans too.

Whichever exciting route you take to owning a Volkswagen campervan, it's going to involve far more decisions and choices than you might imagine. This useful handbook will take you through the processes step-by-step and make sure you end up with the Vee-Dub you've always desired.

Printed in Great Britain
by Amazon